Thomas Ogden

Thomas Ogden: A Contemporary Introduction is the first book to gather and analyse Ogden's significant contributions to contemporary psychoanalytic thinking.

The book meticulously unpacks Ogden's key concepts including the analytic third, reverie, undreamt dreams, and the music of language, demonstrating how these ideas have fundamentally altered contemporary psychoanalytic practice. Through Ofrit Shapira-Berman's detailed analysis of his writings and clinical approach, readers gain practical insights into implementing Ogden's methods while understanding the philosophical underpinnings of his work. Paying close attention to his ontological perspective, Shapira-Berman considers Ogden's unique integration of literary sensibility with clinical wisdom to offer practitioners new ways to engage with patients beyond traditional interpretive frameworks.

Part of the Routledge Introductions to Contemporary Psychoanalysis series, this concise and informative book is essential reading for psychoanalysts, psychotherapists, and clinical psychologists seeking to deepen their therapeutic practice. Graduate students and researchers in psychoanalytic theory will find it an invaluable resource for understanding one of the field's most influential contemporary thinkers.

Ofrit Shapira-Berman is a psychoanalyst working in private practice in Tel-Aviv, Israel, a training analyst at the Tel-Aviv Institute for Contemporary Psychoanalysis, and professor at the Hebrew University. She is the author of *Psychoanalysis and Maternal Absence: From the Traumatic to Faith and Trust* (2022).

Routledge Introductions to Contemporary Psychoanalysis

Series Editor: Aner Govrin
Executive Editor: Yael Peri Herzovich

'Thomas Ogden is arguably the foremost original contemporary psychoanalyst. His voluminous writings never fail to disappoint the reader who searches for emotional clarity about the nature of the analysing situation. Since his early work Ogden has creatively evolved and honed his particular clinical paradigm stemming from his scholarly work on, especially, the work of Freud, Winnicott, Klein and Bion integrated alongside his innovative clinical acumen. The more recent identification of an ontological psychoanalysis, takes Ogden's work to further inspiring peaks that advance psychoanalysis with an authentic depth and without a sacrifice to the foundational authors he follows. On the contrary, their oeuvre is illuminated and enhanced. Reading Ogden is always inspiring and a pleasure. In this volume Ofrit Shapira-Berman has created an impressive Ogdenian psychoanalytic object that is 'waiting to be found and used' by the beginner in psychoanalysis through to the most learned and experienced psychoanalyst. With a finely tuned dedication, rarely seen in secondary sources, Shapira-Berman's dedicated and close reading of Ogden's work takes the reader on a fascinating odyssey of Ogden's remarkable oeuvre.'

Jan Abram, *Psychoanalyst of the British Psychoanalytical Society, Author of The Surviving Object: Psychoanalytic clinical essays on psychic survival-of-the-object (2022) New Library of Psychoanalysis, Routledge*

'Not to know the fresh and deep thinking of Thomas Ogden as well as the lyrical beauty of his writing, appealing eloquence not common in the academic world. His spirit is Freudian in its breadth of curiosity and depth of sensitivity, while his original thinking refreshes old understandings, all expressed in the beauty of uncommonly poetic writing. This short volume can serve as an introduction, a valuable gateway to the contributions I believe to be the most significant in the current psychoanalytic world. Ogden is a delight as he sweeps away the cobwebs in one's mind. Do let Ofrit Shapira Berman introduce him, I have no doubt you will want to get to know him firsthand, you will be richly rewarded by the pleasures of his thinking and writing.'

Warren Poland, author of *Intimacy and Sensitivity in Psychoanalysis*

For more information about this series, please visit: www.routledge.com/Routledge-Introductions-to-Contemporary-Psychoanalysis/book-series/ICP

Thomas Ogden

A Contemporary Introduction

Ofrit Shapira-Berman

Routledge
Taylor & Francis Group

NEW YORK AND LONDON

Designed cover image: Other

First published 2026
by Routledge
605 Third Avenue, New York, NY 10158

and by Routledge
4 Park Square, Milton Park, Abingdon, Oxon OX14 4RN

*Routledge is an imprint of the Taylor & Francis Group, an informa
business*

Library of Congress Cataloging-in-Publication Data
A catalog record for this title has been requested

ISBN: 978-1-032-48373-3 (hbk)
ISBN: 978-1-032-47881-4 (pbk)
ISBN: 978-1-003-38870-8 (ebk)

DOI: 10.4324/9781003388708

Typeset in Times New Roman
by Taylor & Francis Books

In memory of my father (1943–2024)

Contents

Preface

Reading Thomas Ogden changes you. His work seeps into your consciousness gradually, like water into soil, transforming how you think, listen, and be with others. As both readers and practitioners, we find ourselves altered by encountering his ideas—not just intellectually, but in our very way of being present with patients and ourselves. His contributions to psychoanalysis represent more than an evolution in technique; they constitute a fundamental reimagining of what it means to engage in the therapeutic encounter.

At the heart of Ogden's vision lies the concept of 'the analytic third'—that unique intersubjective space that emerges between analyst and patient. Through his careful attention to reverie and the subtle nuances of therapeutic interaction, Ogden shows how this third space becomes the medium through which genuine psychological transformation becomes possible. Rather than primarily seeking to uncover hidden meanings or resolve unconscious conflicts, we work to create conditions where new ways of being become possible. This shift doesn't negate the importance of understanding but places it in service of a larger goal: the development of greater capacity for authentic living and experience.

His work on reverie has fundamentally shifted how many of us experience our own internal processes during sessions. Those fleeting thoughts, memory fragments, bodily sensations, and emotional resonances, which we might once have dismissed as distractions, become valued aspects of the therapeutic process. We learn to trust these experiences, to allow them to inform our understanding without rushing to interpret them. This requires a particular kind of courage—the courage to not know, to stay with uncertainty, to allow meaning to emerge rather than imposing it.

The influence of writers like Borges, Kafka, Frost, and Heaney in Ogden's approach teaches us to see each session as a kind of living text, with multiple layers of meaning unfolding simultaneously. His concept of 'talking-as-dreaming' transforms how we engage with patients—we attend not just to what is said, but to how it is said, to the pauses and silences, to the subtle shifts in tone and rhythm that signal deeper movements in the psyche. Working with 'undreamable experiences' becomes less about technique and more about creating conditions where the previously unthinkable might begin to take shape. We learn to sit with our patients in the darkness of trauma and neglect, trusting that our presence and our willingness to bear witness without rushing to understand or fix can help create space for new possibilities.

In an era dominated by quick fixes and superficial solutions, Ogden's work reminds us of the irreducible complexity of human experience. Through his integration of clinical wisdom, philosophical depth, and literary sensitivity he shows us how psychoanalytic practice can remain vital and relevant while staying true to its deepest insights about human nature. His emphasis on authentic engagement and emotional depth offers invaluable guidance for facing contemporary psychological challenges.

For those of us who deeply engage with his work Ogden becomes more than a theoretical influence—he becomes an internal presence, a voice that helps us stay true to what matters most: the creation of conditions where genuine psychological transformation becomes possible. His legacy lives on not just in his writings but in the countless therapeutic encounters enriched by his insights, in the practitioners who have learned from him how to be more fully present in their work, and in the patients whose lives have been transformed through deeply human engagement. As we look to the future of psychoanalytic practice, Ogden's work reminds us that our most important tool is not our theoretical knowledge or technical skill, but our capacity for genuine human presence—our willingness to engage authentically, to remain open to surprise and uncertainty, and to trust the transformative power of genuine human encounter.

Prof. Ofrit Shapira Berman
Israel
December 2024

Introduction
The Evolution of Thomas Ogden's Ontological Psychoanalysis

Thomas Ogden's work, while primarily using spoken language as an analytical tool, explores experiences that transcend conscious verbal expression. Through his extensive writings on reverie, dreaming, the analytic third, the feeling of real, poetry, and the music of language, Ogden examines human experiences that defy straightforward verbalization. His unique approach has significantly influenced contemporary psychoanalytic thought and practice.

To understand Ogden's distinctive contribution, we must contrast two fundamental approaches in psychoanalytic thought. The first one is the traditional epistemological approach, exemplified by Freud and Klein, emphasizing understanding and interpreting unconscious material—uncovering hidden meanings, analysing defence mechanisms, and making the unconscious conscious. In contrast, the ontological approach, developed by theorists like Bion and Winnicott and further refined by Ogden, focuses on the patient's way of *being* and *becoming*—their capacity to *feel real, alive*, and *authentic in their experience.*

Ogden (2019) describes this shift as a transformation "from epistemological (pertaining to knowing and understanding) psychoanalysis to ontological (pertaining to being and becoming) psychoanalysis" (p. 662). While these approaches are not mutually exclusive, Ogden's work has been distinctly ontological from its inception. He uses the term 'ontological psychoanalysis' to describe an analytical attitude primarily concerned with "creating conditions in which the patient might become more fully alive and real to him- or herself" (2004a, p. 13).

DOI: 10.4324/9781003388708-1

These two dimensions of psychoanalysis exist in a dynamic relationship. As Ogden (2004b) explains, "The ontological dimension of psychoanalysis (coming into being) serves as the matrix within which the epistemological (coming to understand) evolves. Understanding is born of experiencing, but experiencing is not born of understanding. One may come into being in ways that do not involve self-understanding, for instance, in playing, dreaming, writing, and all other creative activities" (p. 14). This perspective challenges traditional notions of psychoanalytic insight and emphasizes the transformative power of lived experience within the analytic relationship. Within ontological psychoanalysis, the analyst takes a relatively non-interpretive position, using *experience and experiencing* as a relatively major 'tool' of transformation. Ogden (1994a) has discussed his idea concerning 'interpretive action' as "the analyst's use of *action* (other than verbally symbolic speech) to convey to the analysand specific aspects of the analyst's understanding of the transference-countertransference which cannot at that juncture in the analysis be conveyed by the semantic *content* of *words alone*" (p. 219, italics added).

Throughout his writing career, Ogden has pursued an elusive quality in psychoanalytic experience. His approach resembles artistic expression more than theoretical prescription, offering neither doctrine nor mere clinical recommendations. Instead, his work embodies a form of creative expression that invites readers to discover new dimensions of themselves and their psychoanalytic practice. His writing style has qualities of literature or poetry, enabling readers to uncover previously unrecognized aspects of their professional and personal understanding.

Ogden has also made significant contributions to understand the experiences of reading and writing, which he sees as parallels to the analytic experience in their capacity for self-discovery and transformation. These activities—reading, writing, and participating in analysis—constitute experiences through which we conceive and reconceive ourselves. As he notes in "Rethinking the concepts of the unconscious and analytic time" (2024b), "In reading a literary text … meaning is not found behind the words or under the words; meaning resides in the words and the effects they create. We listen to the words, not through them" (p. 281).

This principle extends to psychoanalytic practice itself. Even when an analyst offers an interpretation, its essence lies not in *what* is being said, but in the patient's experience of it—what they feel and sense in the moment of interpretation. A concept that remains static, resistant to rediscovery and recreation, becomes what might be termed a dead object. The vitality of an idea depends on our ability and willingness to engage with it playfully, maintaining its relevance to contemporary practice.

Ogden's work has also deeply influenced our understanding of intersubjectivity in the analytic process. His concept of the 'analytic third' describes a third subjectivity created by the unconscious interplay between analyst and analysand. This idea challenges traditional notions of analytic neutrality and emphasizes the co-created nature of the analytic experience.

Furthermore, Ogden's exploration of reverie—the analyst's seemingly irrelevant or distracting thoughts during sessions—has expanded our understanding of countertransference and the analyst's use of self. He posits that these wandering thoughts, far from being obstacles, can provide valuable insights into the patient's unconscious communications and the dynamics of the analytic relationship.

This book traces Ogden's development as a significant psychoanalytic thinker and writer. Although representing just one possible interpretation of his evolution, it aims to provide a systematic examination of his thinking and theoretical progression. Through this exploration, we seek to offer readers a framework for developing their own theoretical understanding while acknowledging the inherent limitations of selecting specific papers from his extensive body of work for detailed analysis.

As we delve into Ogden's work, we will explore how his ideas have evolved over time, their impact on clinical practice, and their implications for the future of psychoanalysis. We will examine key concepts such as 'the analytic third', 'reverie', and the nature of psychoanalytic interpretation, as well as his unique perspectives on the process of reading and writing psychoanalytic texts.

By engaging with Ogden's work in this way, I hope to not only elucidate his contributions to the field but also to encourage readers to engage in their own process of discovery and creative thinking about psychoanalytic theory and practice. In doing so, I aim to address Ogden's emphasis on the transformative power of experience and the ongoing evolution of psychoanalytic thought. The book is divided into four parts:

Part One: Ogden's Original Contributions and Elaborations of Psychoanalytic Concepts

This part of the book examines his development of key concepts such as projective identification, reverie, and the analytic third. These elaborations have expanded the theoretical understanding and practical application of fundamental psychoanalytic ideas, making them more accessible to both theorists and practitioners.

Part Two: Re-Thinking the Psychoanalytic Ancestors—What Is There to Be Re-Found?

This part of the book explores Ogden's distinctive approach to reinterpreting foundational psychoanalytic texts. His careful readings of Freud, Klein, Isaacs, Winnicott, Bion, Loewald, Searles, and Fairbairn offer expanded understanding and creative elaboration of their more ambiguous concepts. Through these reinterpretations, Ogden demonstrates how each generation must recreate theoretical understanding anew, breathing fresh life into established ideas while maintaining their essential truths.

Part Three: Reading, Writing, and Practising Psychoanalysis

This part investigates the integration of these three experiences in Ogden's work. As a discerning reader, skilled writer, and dedicated analyst, Ogden illuminates the complementary nature of these activities, demonstrating how they collectively foster and enhance the capacity for dreaming and creative thought. His examination reveals how each mode of engagement—reading, writing, and analytic work—contributes to the development of psychological understanding and emotional truth.

Part Four: Ontological Psychoanalysis—The Re-Creation and Experiencing of Something (A)New

The last part of the book traces the culmination of Ogden's ontological thinking, beginning with his 2019 paper defining ontological psychoanalysis. This section examines how Ogden synthesizes Winnicott's and Bion's emphasis on patient experience with his own theoretical developments, analysing two additional papers that encapsulate his most valued theoretical-clinical insights. This final section demonstrates how Ogden's work represents a significant transformation in psychoanalytic thinking, shifting emphasis from epistemological understanding to ontological experiencing.

Through systematic examination of Ogden's work, this book aims to illuminate the development of his ontological perspective while providing readers with frameworks for their own theoretical growth and clinical practice. The analysis emphasizes not only the content of Ogden's ideas, but also the process through which he develops them, reflecting his belief that psychoanalytic thinking must remain alive through continuous recreation and personal engagement.

This book's methodology reflects Ogden's own approach to reading and interpretation. Each chapter examines key papers chronologically while identifying thematic connections that emerge across his work. Special attention is paid to Ogden's use of language, his integration of clinical and theoretical insights, and the ways in which his thinking both builds upon and transforms psychoanalytic tradition.

Chapter 1

Ogden's Original Contributions to and Elaborations of Psychoanalytic Concepts

This section examines several of Ogden's seminal papers, in which he interprets and reconceptualizes fundamental psychoanalytic concepts, particularly 'projective identification', 'reverie', and the 'analytic third'. Following the Introduction, I will present Ogden's theoretical perception of these three concepts, and this will be followed by two of Ogden's clinical presentations.

Introduction

One of Ogden's earliest papers, "On projective identification" (1979a), introduced Klein's concept and theoretical thinking to the American audience. Until then, Klein was almost absent from psychoanalytic thinking and publication, virtually ignored by most American psychoanalysts besides Grotstein (1980a, 1980b, 1981), who had not published a paper on this concept. Ogden, who is not a 'Kleinian', hence free from Kleinian 'ideology', redefined Klein's concept as a process that can be divided into 'phases'. Although no such 'phases' exist, this sub-division helps readers and clinicians to better understand and utilize this thinking in their clinical work.

The second concept originally developed by Ogden is the 'analytic third.' Ogden and André Green are the only psychoanalysts who have written about this concept, and their perceptions of it are different and should be distinguished. Ogden's analytic third builds on his understanding and re-conceptualization of projective identification as a particular form of intersubjectivity. In a later

DOI: 10.4324/9781003388708-2

paper ("The perverse subject of analysis", 1996), Ogden elaborates his thinking concerning the analytic third, referring to the analyst's ability to remain emotionally alive. Even at that point, Ogden was concerned with the issue of aliveness—deadness within the analytic session. Much of Ogden's writing refers to Winnicott's papers and theoretical thinking, specifically on the meaning and essence of being alive, adding to Winnicott's thinking his own original perception of the ways in which psychoanalysis can help people become more fully alive and real to themselves and recover what he calls "unlived life" (Ogden, 2016a).

The third concept that Ogden has developed extensively, making it the anchor of both his theoretical thinking and clinical work, is 'reverie'. Ogden's conceptualization of Bion's (1970) reverie can be viewed as a transformation; for Ogden, reverie encompasses the analyst's most mundane thoughts, feelings, sensations, and recollections of daily experiences. These experiences can easily be perceived as distractions, hence causing the analyst to feel ashamed and embarrassed of not being with the patient in the here-and-now of the session. Yet Ogden argues the opposite, referring to the analyst's reveries as being with him/herself and the patient simultaneously, allowing an unconscious experience to emerge that is both personal and individual, as well as mutually interconnected.

These three concepts are among Ogden's most valuable contributions to modern psychoanalytic thinking. Projective identification, the 'analytic third', and the analyst's use of reveries are all mutually created by the patient and the analyst in the psychic space that is created by 'both' and 'neither'. Ogden (1985) conceptualizes the relationship between these subjectivities as existing within "dialectic dialogue" or "tension": "A dialectical process is one in which two opposing concepts each creates, informs, preserves, and negates the other, each standing in a dynamic (ever-changing) relationship with the other" (p. 130). He further elaborates: "The dialectical process moves toward integration, but integration is never complete; each integration creates a new dialectical opposition and a new dynamic tension" (p. 131).

These three concepts are paradoxical in the sense that they are at once intra-psychic (one-person psychology) and inter-personal (two-persons psychology). Ogden (1985) suggests that the potential space between mother and infant (or analyst and patient) embodies an unchallenged paradox: "The infant and mother are one, and the infant and mother are two" (p. 132). It is within this 'space' that one's being, creativity, and thinking are generated. Ogden (1979a) positions "being" and "aliveness" within this potential space, a "hypothetical area that exists (but cannot exist) between the baby and the object (mother or part of mother) during the phase of the repudiation of the object as not-me, that is, at the end of being merged in with the object" (Winnicott, 2007, p. 107). This is perpetually paradoxical.

Ogden's definitions of 'projective identification', 'reverie' and 'the analytic third' are multifaceted, describing phenomena that belong to this potential space that is at once *within the individual* (patient or analyst) and *intersubjective*. The dialectical tension is present in other features of these three concepts. Projective identification, for example, helps patients distance themselves from aspects of their experience that are too frightening and confusing, but at the same time allows them to be in touch with those experiences. Reverie is simultaneously the analyst's way of being with him/herself, and his way of being with the patient, in a very specific manner. For me, one's ability to be connected emotionally to as many aspects of reverie experience as possible is fundamental to being *fully alive* with the patient.

Ogden's Projective Identification

In his analysis of projective identification (1979a), Ogden offers a conceptualization that is based on a bidirectional movement between internal and external, fantasy and reality. Neither member of these pairs can fully exist without the other. Ogden builds upon Bion's conceptualization of projective identification (1959) as a form of communication between two people, which is both unconscious and conscious, both intra-psychic and intersubjective.

Initially, this form of communication (e.g., projective identification) requires a 'real' maternal object external to the baby yet sufficiently immersed in the baby's internal experience to be able to communicate with the baby, and some aspect (a feeling, a bodily sensation) that the baby cannot contain by itself. By 'real' mother I am referring to a mother whose subjectivity is rich and stable enough for her to be able to suspend it (and *use it*) in a way that allows her to be preoccupied with her baby. Such preoccupation with the baby allows the mother to experience and actively contain the baby's experience. Following the active containing, the mother can communicate the 'digested' material to the baby, in ways that are less frightening to it. This delicate process demands for the mother to be *fully alive*, that is, a subject in her own right.

Ogden (1979b) thinks of Bion's definition of projective identification as akin to the experience of "having a thought without a thinker" (p. 365), and he conceptualizes projective identification in a way that is related to his conceptualization of reverie in multiple ways. Ogden states: "I conceive of the analytic process as involving the creation of unconscious intersubjective events that have never previously existed in the affective life of either analyst or analysand" (p. 589).

However, I propose that this statement warrants further examination. Rather than suggesting entirely new creations, I argue that these intersubjective experiences represent novel configurations of elements that have existed unconsciously within patient, analyst, or both. The unconscious elements find new expressions through their joint creation within the analytic relationship, expressing themselves in new forms. The patient's capacity to re-experience some of their most traumatic (past) experiences within the analytic relationship is the bedrock of psychoanalysis, both theoretically and clinically.

Both 'projective identification' and reverie are rooted in *experience* and *experiencing;* they emerge from the unconscious and are manifested through physical and emotional associations that may initially appear nonsensical. The analyst may feel bored, or 'distracted' or find him/herself preoccupied with some mundane detail (e.g., when is the garage going to close today, or the way his address is written on an envelope). Following this thought (or image, or a bodily sensation), the analyst may notice certain emotions, or other memories, feelings, bodily sensations. All these emotional, cognitive, or bodily experiences belong to a complex, multi-layered analytic space and are, in certain ways, co-creations of the analyst and the patient. One must develop a capacity to make use of these co-created phenomena, which takes time and much experience.

Projective Identification (and Reverie) in Ogden's Clinical Presentation

In his paper "On projective identification" Ogden (1979a) presents a few clinical illustrations of projective identification, out of which I chose the following about Mr. J:

> Mr J had been a patient in analysis for about a year and the treatment seemed to both patient and analyst to be bogging down. The patient repetitively questioned whether he was 'getting anything out of it', 'maybe it's a waste of time', etc. Mr J had always grudgingly paid his bills, but gradually they were being paid later and later, leaving the analyst to wonder whether the bill was going to be paid at all. The analyst found himself questioning whether the patient might drop out of treatment, leaving that month's and the previous month's bills unpaid. Also, as the sessions dragged on, the analyst thought about colleagues who held fifty-minute sessions instead of fifty-five-minute ones and charged the same fee as this analyst. Just before the beginning of one session, the analyst considered shortening the 'hour' by making the patient wait a couple of minutes before letting him into the office. All of this occurred without attention being focused on it either by the patient or the analyst. Gradually, the analyst found himself having difficulty ending the sessions on time because of an intensely guilty feeling that he was not giving the patient 'his money's worth'. After this difficulty with time repeated itself again and again over several months, the analyst was gradually able to begin to understand his trouble in maintaining the ground rules of the analysis. It began to be apparent to the analyst that he had been feeling greedy for expecting to be paid for his 'worthless' work and was defending himself against such feelings by being so generous with his time that no one could accuse him of greed. With this understanding of the feelings that were being engendered in him by the patient,

the analyst was able to take a fresh look at the patient's material. Mr J's father had deserted him and his mother when the patient was 15 months old. His mother, without ever explicitly saying so, had held the patient responsible for this. The unspoken, shared feeling was that it was the patient's greediness for the mother's time, energy and affection that had resulted in the father's desertion. The patient developed an intense need to disown and deny feelings of greed. He could not tell the analyst that he wished to meet more frequently because he experienced this wish as greediness that would result in abandonment by the (transference) father and in attack by the (transference) mother that he saw in the analyst. Instead, the patient insisted that the analysis and the analyst were totally undesirable and worthless. The interaction with the analyst subtly engendered in the analyst intense feelings of a type of greed that was felt to be so unacceptable to the analyst that the analyst at first also tried to deny and disown it. For the analyst, the first step in integration of the feeling of greediness was the ability to register a perception of himself experiencing guilt and defending himself against his feelings of greed. He could then mobilize an aspect of himself that was interested in understanding his greedy and guilty feelings, rather than trying to deny, disguise, displace or project them. Essential for this aspect of psychological work was the ana-lyst's feeling that he could have greedy and guilty feelings without being damaged by them.

(pp. 362–3)

This clinical illustration already shows Ogden's deep under-standing of the analytic process and his ability to use his own reveries (i.e., when wondering whether the patient will leave the analysis without paying or wandering off to think about his col-leagues and their management of the analytic session) in his clin-ical work. His statement that it was not the analyst's greediness per se that was encumbering the psychic-emotional progress, but rather his disavowing them, refers not only to Klein's theory of projective identification but to his own concern with what allows patients (and analysts) to *be more alive, together and separately.*

Although this paper was written years before Ogden developed his theoretical understanding of utilizing reveries as part of creating the analytic third with the patient, the roots of these ideas can already be detected in his 1979 paper. As often is the case with artistic creations, (as well as with psychoanalytic work), the roots are more easily identified in retrospect.

Projective identifications and reveries allow patients and analysts to enter various aspects of their experience that cannot (yet) be verbalized. In this sense, they act similarly to 'dreams' and 'dreaming' - it is a story that patients and analysts need to know about, through *experience* and *experiencing* before it can be put into words. I often think about reverie as playing, or approaching a riddle in a way that is similar to our way of approaching a dream. What is most interesting about it is not what is clear, but rather what we can make of it with someone else's help, whether that "someone else" is another person or a part of ourselves who can analyse our own dream. The two ideas are strongly connected to Ogden's theory of the analytic third—a (potential, intermediate) 'space', in which a new psychic-emotional experience is mutually created by analyst and patient, belonging to one of them, both, or neither of them. It is a paradoxical 'space', in which the lines, between the analyst's and the patient's experience, cannot (and should not) be determined clearly.

Working with the 'Analytic Third'—Clinical Illustration

In his paper "The analytic third: Implications for psychoanalytic theory and technique", Ogden (2004c) presents a fragment of an analysis in which he illustrates his way of utilizing his reveries. Ogden finds himself (as if) wandering off, thinking about some scribbling on an envelope in his office. Through Ogden's detailed description of his thoughts we get a rare chance to be an audience to some of the most private thoughts that may cross an analyst's mind while the patient lies on the couch. These thoughts could easily cause the analyst to feel guilty or embarrassed as they may be experienced as being lost within his/her own internal world. We may be tempted to brush them away, feeling we are not fulfilling our 'duty' to be completely attentive to the patient. Yet Ogden invites us to not only be attentive to the patient's associations, but also to our own. Reveries are the analyst's own associations, and they often carry great significance. Ogden retrieves himself out of his reverie and soon realizes that:

> I was feeling suspicious about the genuineness of the intimacy that the letter had seemed to convey. My fleeting fantasy that the letter had been part of a bulk mailing reflected a feeling that I had been duped. I felt that I had been naive and gullible, ready to believe that I was being entrusted with a special secret.
>
> (p. 171)

Upon listening to his patient, Ogden has an emotional experience of his patient's way of talking:

> I was aware that he was talking in a way that was highly characteristic of him—he sounded weary and hopeless and yet was doggedly trudging on in his production of 'free associations'. He had during the entire period of the analysis been struggling mightily to escape the confines of his extreme emotional detachment from himself and from other people. I thought of Mr. L's description of his driving up to the house in which he lives and not being able to feel that it was his house. When he walked inside, he was greeted by 'the woman and four children who lived there', but could not feel that they were his wife and his children.
>
> (p. 171)

This allows for a 'new' acknowledgement of the patient's dreams, being full of images of "paralyzed people, prisoners, and mutes" (p. 172). Ogden assumes a connection between the patient's tone of voice, references to his wife and children, dreams and overall emotional detachment, and his own reverie in that session, in which he feels betrayed by his preliminary belief that the letter was specifically written to him, only to realize that it was sent to many people. This experience of being betrayed by an unfulfilled promise for intimacy opened options for new emotional experiences in the analysis of Mr. L. The analyst's ability to experience an aspect of his own internal world is vital to his ability to live an experience together with the patient, an experience that is at the same time individual and personal, as well as mutual and jointly created.

Emphasizing the vital analytic importance of experience and experiencing what cannot (and perhaps should not) be verbalized (yet), Ogden stresses that:

> The experience of reverie is rarely, if ever, 'translatable' in a one-to-one fashion into an understanding of what is going on in the analytic relationship. The attempt to make immediate interpretive use of the affective or ideational content of our reveries usually leads to superficial interpretations in which manifest content is treated as interchangeable with latent content.

(Ogden, 1997c, p. 569)

Summary

Ogden's interpretation of Klein's concept of projective identification and Bion's (1970) concept of reverie, and his own original conception of the analytic third are to be understood as an often inseparable 'threesome'. In the introduction to his paper ("The analytic third: Implications for psychoanalytic theory and practice"), Ogden (2004c, 2018a) writes:

> I will offer a reconsideration of the phenomenon of projective identification and its role in the analytic process by viewing it as a form of the intersubjective analytic third. In projective identification, as I understand it, the individual subjectivities of both analyst and analysand are to a large extent subsumed by a third subject of analysis, an unconscious, co-created one: the *subjugating third*. A successful analytic experience involves a superseding of the third by means of mutual recognition of analyst and analysand as separate subjects and a reappropriation of the (transformed) individual subjectivities of the participants.

(p. 169)

Throughout his work, Ogden elaborates on the theoretical significance and the clinical implementations of the analyst's and patient's ability to make use of his/her dreams and reveries, balancing the paradoxes of mutually creating something that is both 'old' and 'new', and of being 'immersed' in something which, although it is shared, remains utterly personal and individual.

Chapter 2

Re-Thinking the Psychoanalytic Ancestors— What Is There to Be Re-Found?

In this chapter I will refer to seven of Ogden's papers dedicated to his psychoanalytic predecessors. Following his year at the Tavistock clinic, Ogden returned to the USA fascinated with British psychoanalytic writers (especially Winnicott and Bion) and then played a crucial role in making traditional British psychoanalysis accessible to American audiences.

Beginning with Klein's and Isaacs' thinking on the 'unconscious fantasy', through his extensive engagement with Winnicott's and Bion's papers and Fairbairn's theory of internal objects, Ogden developed a distinctive theoretical perspective, influencing not only the theoretical thinking of other psychoanalysts but also modern psychoanalytic technique. His definition of 'a life worth living', as well as 'psychoanalysis worth pursuing', appears to be grounded in two fundamental aspects: (1) being and (2) thinking. These elements are connected through the medium of dreaming, and Ogden offers his readers some new analytic definitions, carefully weaving and reconstructing them as 'states of mind', 'psycho-emotional functions', 'analytic aims', and 'achievements.'

The first two papers I will examine are Klein's and Isaac's contributions concerning the idea of 'unconscious phantasy'. This will be followed by a discussion of "Reading Winnicott" (2001), and of Ogden's "On not being able to dream" (2003) and "On holding and containing, being and dreaming" (2004d). In these papers, Ogden weaves together Winnicott's and Bion's thinking, positioning them on the same continuum regarding 'being', 'dreaming','

DOI: 10.4324/9781003388708-3

and 'thinking'. Connecting Winnicott with Bion is rather unusual within psychoanalytic writing; most often it is Klein and Bion who go together. Lastly, I will discuss Ogden's "An introduction to the reading of Bion" (2004a) and "Intuiting the truth of what's happening: On Bion's 'Notes on memory and desire'" (2015). Ogden has given his unique analysis of additional psychoanalytic ancestors (e.g., "Reading Harold Searles" (2007), "Why read Fairbairn" (2010)), but given the limitations, I will only refer, in addition to the papers I have mentioned, to Ogden's paper "Reading Loewald: Oedipus reconceived" (2006), as I find it to provide a possible explanation for Ogden's dedication to recreating many of the ideas of his ancestors.

Loewald's paper (1979) offers a revolutionary reconceptualization of Freud's oedipal theory, to which Ogden adds his own third-generation creativity. Adding to Loewald's perspective on the oedipal struggle, Ogden emphasizes three fundamental ideas: (1) the tension between parental influence and the child's innate need to establish independent capacities for originality lies at the core of the Oedipus complex; (2) the idea that oedipal parricide is driven fundamentally by the child's urge for emancipation, involving both revolt against and appropriation of parental authority; and (3) the idea that the child atones for parricide by internalizing a transformed version of their experience of the oedipal parents.

For Ogden, the oedipal killing of one's parents *need not be murderous* but rather *represents an act of becoming and emancipation*. Growing up requires 'killing off' one's parents in the sense of gaining permission to have one's own dreams and thoughts. Furthermore, parents and ancestors must be willing to 'be killed', allowing the torch to be passed on to the next generation. Though never easy, this process proves crucial for life's continuation. Each generation must be permitted to find what has been found before and recreate ideas anew. In recreating and transforming some of the ideas of his psychoanalytic ancestors, Ogden does *not* eliminate their ideas, but rather steps forward to take up his own, unique, *emancipated position, becoming a theorist in his own right.*

Discussing Ogden's "Instinct, Phantasy, and Psychological Deep Structure—A Reinterpretation of Aspects of the Work of Melanie Klein" (1984) and "Reading Susan Isaacs: Towards a Radically Revised Theory of Thinking" (2011)

Although Ogden has written several papers on Freud's thinking, Klein's theory appears particularly significant to his effort in making some of the British school's theories and concepts accessible to American audiences. Klein's ideas about the death drive were (and still are) controversial and so are her ideas about the very first phases of life and the ability to treat young infants psychoanalytically, but Ogden focuses on her conceptualization of the 'unconscious fantasy' and its significance. The two papers he dedicated to this concept refer to both Klein and Isaacs, suggesting that rather than merely *explaining* Klein's theoretical framework, Isaacs made an *original contribution, expanding* Klein's theory in distinctive ways. More than two decades separate the two papers, allowing us, the readers, to trace possible changes in Ogden's own thinking.

In 1984, Ogden's paper focused primarily on introducing Klein's drive theory to the American professional audience, who, at that time, were steeped in ego psychology.

By 2011, when his second paper on Isaacs' contribution was published, ,Ogden was already deeply engaged with Winnicott's and Bion's thinking, laying the groundwork for his recent distinction between *epistemological* psychoanalysis (represented by Freud and Klein) and *ontological* psychoanalysis (represented by Winnicott and Bion). Through this distinction, Ogden marks the transformation from psychoanalysis focused on 'knowing' and 'understanding' to psychoanalysis centred on 'being' and 'experiencing'.

"Instinct, phantasy, and psychological deep structure—A reinterpretation of aspects of the work of Melanie Klein" reveals Ogden's ambivalence toward Klein's thinking by choosing to open his paper on Klein's thinking with a quotation from Winnicott:

> If you are applying psychoanalytic treatment to children, you should meet Melanie Klein... She is saying some things that

may or not be true, and you must find out for yourself for you
will not get what Melanie Klein teaches in my analysis with you.
(Winnicott, 1962, p. 173)

This opening quotation reveals Ogden's perspective on Klein's theoretical framework: her ideas merit serious consideration, particularly
for child analysts, yet require individual verification through clinical
experience. This stance appears to stem from Klein's emphasis on the
death drive, which Ogden finds challenging. It is her deep understanding of the 'unconscious fantasy' that matters the most for him.
When Ogden writes that "Klein's ideas and the reaction against
them constitute a good deal of the dialogue underlying the development of object relations theory" (p. 500), he illustrates his own conception of a 'dialectical dialogue'—suggesting that theoretical
advancement often emerges out of 'dialectical tension' (i.e., dis-
agreements) rather than from agreement.

Ogden's significant contribution in this paper lies in his application of Chomsky's (1957, 1968) concept of 'deep structure' to
the theory of the 'unconscious fantasy'. He first addresses Klein's
concept of 'fantasy', which he defines as *"the psychic representation of one's biology"* (p. 500). By suggesting that the Id bears
responsibility for transforming the biological/physical into the
phantasmatic, Ogden creates an interesting connection between
Freud, Klein, and Winnicott, particularly concerning the relationship between 'psyche' and 'soma',' suggesting that "The newborn infant's world at the outset is a bodily world, and phantasy
represents the infant's attempts at transforming somatic events
into a mental form" (p. 500).

This formulation suggests a cyclical movement: The infant's
world is, at large, a bodily world (physical/Id), yet the Id, as the
"mind's functional unit", (p. 500, italics added) *bears responsibility
for transforming bodily experiences into mental form through
phantasy.* Ogden bases this idea on Freud's definition of instinct as
'the demand made [by the body] upon the mind for work' (Freud,
1915, p. 168), emphasizing the unbreakable connection between
psyche and soma. Throughout our lives, Ogden argues, phantasies
maintain their connection to our biology and bodily sensations.
Phantasies always carry traces of our instincts, which are

manifested in specific operational modes often perceived as essential to identity.

Ogden addresses a common major disagreement with Kleinian thinking: the possibility that it implies that babies are born with inherited thoughts (via instincts and the Id) and the capacity to think them. He suggests that resistance to this theoretical position stems from two main objections: first, that thoughts derive from experience, and second, that Piaget demonstrated the developmental nature of thinking ability.

Ogden encourages his readers to examine Klein's revolutionary ideas more patiently (specifically her statement that babies are born with inherited thoughts via instincts and the id), using Isaacs to make Klein's concepts more accessible. Isaacs, attempting to clarify Klein's theory, argues for "*the existence of inherited knowledge embedded within bodily impulses that act as* 'vehicles of instincts'" (Isaacs, 1952, p. 93, italics added). While the instinct has an aim and creates physical excitation, carrying knowledge, the baby has not yet experienced what the 'unconscious phantasies' contain within them.

Let me use Isaacs example of a newborn's first encounter with the breast. The infant's ability to seek nourishment often appears miraculous. Yet, according to Isaacs, this 'miracle' (merely) represents "phylogenetic inheritance" (Isaacs, 1952, pp. 117). Such an 'explanation' significantly expands Klein's definition of Freud's instinct, defining it as a mechanism that goes beyond being a 'function' of discharging tension, transforming it into a concept that serves object relatedness. Through this reformulation, Ogden suggests that Isaacs, in explaining Klein's thinking, performs a delicate theoretical dance: One foot is anchored in Freud's thinking, the other in Klein's theoretical evolution, transforming 'instinct theory' into a theory of 'object relations', laying the foundations of Winnicott's later developments.

Ogden appears to agree with Klein that the 'unconscious fantasy' is the deepest psychological structure, yet finds her description of the development of the infant's ability to think to be insufficient, basing it on the rather amorphous concept of "phylogenetic inheritance" (Klein, 1952). Ogden bases the 'unconscious fantasy' on Chomsky's (1957, 1968) theory of linguistic deep structure. According to Chomsky's theory, any (cognitively) healthy infant can learn existing languages, but this requires an inborn ability to make sense of surrounding sounds. This ability, which Ogden refers to as a 'code' (or more precisely, the infant's ability to decode and interpret sounds by attributing meaning), corresponds to Chomsky's term 'deep structure'. Ogden draws comparisons between the 'unconscious fantasy' in infancy and the acquiring of language: An infant does not create linguistic grammar independently, nor is he/she born with the ability to speak or comprehend language. However, *the infant is born with a pre-existing deep structure that enables him/her to attribute meaning to surrounding sounds in ways that develop into language comprehension.* The same is true for the existence of inborn unconscious fantasies.

Ogden (1984) argues that according to this perspective, a baby is not born with the ability to think, but that instead his "knowledge …inherent in bodily impulses" (Isaacs, 1952, p. 94) can be understood "*not as inherited thoughts*, but as a biological code that is an integral part of instinct" (p. 503, italics in original).

Ogden transforms Klein's idea, suggesting that: "the infant might be thought of as born with a powerful predisposition to organize and to make sense of experience along specific lines" (p. 503).

Klein theorizes that the baby's 'unconscious fantasies' as preceding the baby's experiences. Ogden disagrees with her, suggesting that: "In the beginning, phantasy is the infant's interpretation of experience" (p. 503). This change is crucial, as it makes, once again, one's experience and ways of *experiencing* the focal point of one's psychic life and analytic work. Yet, Ogden's transformation of Klein's theoretical conceptualization does consider her perception of both drives:

> Using the paradigm of codes analogous to the deep structure of language, I would restate Klein's ideas in the following way: the relative constitutional endowment of life and death instincts has the major role in determining which code the infant will predominantly rely upon to interpret experience. Experience interpreted in accord with the death instinct will be attributed aggressive and dangerous meanings, while experience organized in terms of the life instinct will be understood in terms of nurturing, loving meanings.
>
> (p. 504)

In this reconceptualization, Ogden refers to both drives, but adds, in his reference to the death drive, an important footnote referencing Grotstein's (1984) proposed understanding of the death drive, "not as a cauldron of destructive impulses (Klein, 1952), nor as the psychological correlate of entropy (Freud, 1920), but *as a system of inborn schemata serving to orient the individual to potential danger*" (Ogden 1984, p. 504).

Ogden emphasizes that actual experiences, while important, do not solely determine the meaning attributed to them. Meanings are shaped by the inborn constitution of drives ('life' and 'death'), which serve as the deep psychological structure of each individual. It is important to note that for him, it is the experience that may (or may not) support "an instinctual mode of organizing experience but does not create the mode by which the experience is interpreted" (p. 504), adding that: "Actual deprivation will confirm the infant's readiness to experience his object as dangerous. The sense of danger is not created by the deprivation; real danger simply confirms the infant's anticipation that such danger exists" (p. 505).

A pre-born code (deep structure) is not (yet) a 'thought' or an 'idea'—it is only the *potential* for such. Having a thought, thinking, and the attribution of meanings demand one's ability to 'symbolize', all of which are related to one's *subjectivity.* Isaacs' proposition that the baby's 'unconscious fantasy' of tearing the mother's breast apart "should be understood as inherent to his/her instincts" (p. 507) is an elaboration of Klein's original theoretical assumption. Whereas Klein puts all her weight on inborn drives, preceding and determining the meaning that the baby will attribute to actual experiences, Ogden reverses the sequence, suggesting that it is the actual experience that will trigger the meaning that the baby attributes, based on the specific equilibrium of his/her drives.

Ogden emphasizes that properly understanding Klein requires recognizing that she defines phantasy not in terms of symbolism (based on the infant's ability to use language through visual or verbal symbols), but rather as *experiences* "borne by sensation and affect" (Isaacs, 1952, p. 92). While this concept proves challenging for adults who think in symbols and communicate through words,

Ogden suggests this theoretical difficulty parallels other psycho-analytic concepts: "The fact that infantile phantasy is not directly observable poses no greater theoretical problem than the concept of the unconscious mind itself which is unobservable. As with the unconscious, all that is observable about infantile phantasy are its derivatives" (Ogden, 1984, p. 510).

Ogden moves to examine the crucial issue of subjectivity, posing an essential question:

> We must inquire into the way in which the Kleinians conceive of the place of the subject in relation to his signs and symbols in the process of re-presenting bodily experience in phantasy. In other words, one must attempt to understand how Klein conceived of the way in which the infant experiences himself in relation to his thoughts and sensations.
>
> (p. 510)

Ogden suggests that Klein's preliminary answer regarding sub-jectivity might lie in "the way in which the infant experiences himself in relation to his thoughts and sensations". However, he proposes that Klein leaves a fundamental question unaddressed:

> Is there a subjective self feeling frightened of bad objects and feeling protected by good ones; or is it simply a fact (experi-enced by no one in particular) that there is danger posed by bad objects, and a fact that there is a need for protection by good objects.
>
> (p. 511)

Subjectivity, Ogden argues, requires a feeling of 'I-ness'—a sense, experience, or experiencing of one's sensations, emotions, and thoughts. This necessitates an I that simultaneously functions as observer and creator. Drawing on his skills as a linguistic analyst, Ogden concludes that Klein does not perceive the infant, at life's beginning, as a subject. He derives this conclusion from Klein's use of the passive voice when discussing the infant's primary object relations.

Many Kleinian writers (including Bick, 1968; Bion, 1962a; Meltzer, 1975; Segal, 1957; and Tustin, 1972) seem to perceive the infant as an independent entity, possessing a *subjectivity*, from early on. Ogden disputes this perspective, preferring Winnicott's declaration that an infant can only be perceived within the unit of mother-infant:

> The infant's thoughts, feelings and perceptions are conceived of by these followers of Klein as constituting things in themselves, events that simply occur. The infant does not experience himself as having a point of view or perspective. There is no infant as thinker or interpreter of his experience.
>
> (pp. 511–512)

Ogden views subjectivity as an achievement that should not be taken for granted. Hence, Isaacs perception of the role and function that 'unconscious fantasy' has in terms of one's ability to attribute meaning to one's experiences, is more suitable: "The process that creates meaning, and that phantasy is the form in which all meanings—including feelings, defence 'mechanisms,' impulses, bodily experiences" emerge (Ogden, 2011, p. 925).

Ogden identifies three crucial elaborations of Isaacs' theoretical ideas: (1) phantasying generates not only unconscious psychic content but constitutes the entirety of unconscious thinking; (2) transference functions as a form of phantasying that enables thinking for the first time (in relation to the analyst) emotional events that occurred in the past but were too disturbing to be experienced when they occurred; and (3) a principal aim and function of phantasy involves fulfilling the human need to understand the truth of one's experience.

By focusing on the ongoing ability to phantasy, Ogden applies Winnicott's seminal contribution to psychoanalytic thinking and practice—the emphasis on '-ing' rather than on a thought as a *static entity;* it is the (a)live movement that matters. Ogden views Isaacs' paper as revolutionary and pivotal in two aspects: (1) marking the evolution of psychoanalysis from Freud's structural model to the model of internal object relations and (2) articulating ideas that Bion would later develop into a comprehensive theory of *thinking*. When first published, Isaacs' theoretical thinking was ahead of its time and Ogden suggests that she *"did not know that she knew"* (p. 926, italics added), referencing the vital role of *'unconscious thinking'*. Often, argues Ogden, it is one's ability to be engaged in psychological processes, which is more significant than their content; the capacity for experiencing, feeling, dreaming, and phantasying constitute what it means to be *fully alive*.

For Ogden the unit mother-infant (analyst-patient) is the unit within which all these processes can occur. Isaacs (like most Kleinians) views "the infant's mental life as operating 'within the infant'" (Ogden, 2011, p. 928), although Isaacs (1952) acknowledges environmental impact on the infant's internal world by emphasizing "the importance of observing both 'precise details' (p. 70) and 'context' (p. 71) for making inferences regarding the infant's internal world and its mental processes" (Ogden, 2011, p. 928). This emphasis on context dialogues with Winnicott's theoretical thinking about the infant-mother unit, although Isaacs is *not* 'Winnicottian'; for her, 'context' refers to the infant's responding to maternal care, yet the mother is not perceived as an object that "actively participates with the infant in generating the infant's internal life" (p. 928). This follows a key difference between Klein's and Winnicott's thinking regarding *differentiation*: For Klein, differentiation exists from life's beginning, while for Winnicott, the baby's development roots in the undifferentiated baby-mother unit, which he calls the mother's primary maternal preoccupation.

Ogden (2011) uses Bion's thinking and reconceptualization of projective identification, to bridge Klein's and Winnicott's thinking:

> There is no such thing as an infant [apart from the maternal provision]" (Winnicott, 1960. pp. 39), while Bion's bridge (1959) potentially lies in his reconceptualization of Klein's projective identification "as an *unconscious, psychological-interpersonal process through which mother and infant engage in thinking together (while remaining separate entities)* beginning in earliest infancy.
>
> (Ogden, 2011, p. 928, italics added)

Connecting ideas require the differentiation between them and Ogden delineates differences and interfaces between Isaacs' thinking and that of Bion and Winnicott:

> Isaacs's understanding of infantile phantasy is cast almost entirely in terms of a conception of the mind of the infant as a system independent of, but responsive to, the workings of the mind of the mother. For Bion, Rosenfeld and Winnicott, as well as those influenced by their revision of the analytic conception of the mind of the infant, the development of the psychological life of the infant is conceived not only in terms of the individual maturational advances of the infant, but also in terms of a psyche jointly created by mother and infant.
>
> (p. 928)

Ogden favours Isaacs' theoretical thinking over Klein's, finding it clearer and richer: "This understanding of the role of phantasy (more accurately, *phantasying*) in unconscious psychological life constitutes a turning point in the development of analytic theory" (p. 929).

For Isaacs:

> All 'mental processes' and 'mental mechanisms' function as forms of *unconscious phantasying*. In other words, mental operations and mechanisms are not impersonal operations ... the various 'mental mechanisms,' such as the defence mechanisms described by Anna Freud (1936), are now viewed as personal psychological creations: 'particular sorts of phantasy' (Isaacs, 1952, p. 78) unique to each individual.
>
> (Ogden, 2011, p. 929)

The most important concept for me in this quote is that of 'phantasying', and I perceive it to be one of the most significant differences between Klein's 'unconscious fantasy' and Isaac's 'unconscious phantasying'; the latter marking an ongoing, dynamic state, unlike the static nature of the first. Unconscious fantasy, states Isaacs (1952), is the base for the patient's relation to the analyst, meaning that transference is the "the chief instrument of learning what is going on in the patient's mind, as well as of discovering or reconstructing his early history" (p. 79). Ogden (2011) concludes that:

> If transference is phantasying, and phantasying is unconscious thinking, then transference holds significance not simply as a symbolic expression of internal object relationships originating in infancy and childhood. In addition, *transference, as I understand it, constitutes a way of thinking for the first time (in relation to the analyst) an emotional situation that occurred in the past. Transference, from this perspective, is inherently more verb than noun, that is, it comprises an effort to think disturbing experiences with the analyst that had previously been unthinkable.*
>
> (p. 930, italics added)

For me, a major idea that Ogden brings forward is the role of transference in facilitating the patient's (and perhaps also the analyst's) ability to experience and think what was until then unthinkable. Another dramatic idea is articulated next, reflecting Ogden's identity not only as a psychoanalyst, but also as a writer, demonstrating the junction between linguistics, grammar, and clinical theory: "*Transference, from this perspective, is inherently more verb than noun*, that is, it comprises an effort to think disturbing experiences with the analyst that had previously been unthinkable" (p. 930, italics added).

Through this reconceptualization of Isaacs' pivotal contribution, Ogden creatively combines Isaacs' thinking with Winnicott's, reconstructing transference in a new form imprinting, which will, years later, become his theory of 'ontological psychoanalysis'; defining transference as a verb, reconstructing it as an *experience* allowing the *becoming* of the patient. The transference allows the patient to *experience* something that has happened years ago, that he/she was unable to experience, or think about until that became possible within the patient-analyst unit. Ogden is making a reference to Winnicott's theoretical concept of 'fear of breakdown' demonstrating his distinctive analytical approach as a theorist and a writer—that is, his ability to weave together different writers and their thinking, creating something new, of his own. Ogden connects Isaacs' reconceptualization of transference as unconscious phantasy to Winnicott's concept of fear of breakdown:

> Fear of psychological collapse that has already occurred much earlier in the patient's life (usually in infancy or childhood). When the breakdown occurred, the individual was not psychologically able (even with the help of his parents) to 'encompass something' (Winnicott, 1974, p. 91), to take in what was occurring.
>
> (Ogden, 2014, p. 930)

Ogden contributes to our understanding of Winnicott's theory concerning the patient's 'fear of breakdown', which does not refer to a repressed traumatic experience, but to *experiences that occurred during developmental phases when the infant lacked subjectivity*, relying, instead, on maternal holding and containing of these unbearable experiences. These frightening experiences can be experienced, in fact for the first time, within the safety of the analytic relationship. This understanding leads Ogden to another reconceptualization:

> Transference activity, from this perspective, is *a psychological act*, not of re-living infantile and childhood experience, rather, it is the opposite of a repetition of early experience— it is an act of experiencing for the first time (with the analyst and in relation to the analyst) an emotional event that occurred in infancy or childhood, but was impossible to experience at the time.
>
> (pp. 930, italics added)

In this formulation, Ogden articulates several theoretical ideas:

1   Transference is not merely repetition of early object relations but also a new creation, particular to a specific patient-analyst unit. Like each mother-infant unit that creates something uniquely specific, each analyst-patient pair develops their distinctive way of working.

2   There exists mutual interdependence between any dyad, oper-
    ating non-linearly. Isaacs can influence our understanding of
    Winnicott's thinking just as Winnicott may influence our
    reading of Isaacs. This backwards movement, from present to
    past, becomes possible because for Ogden, each reader and
    reading represents a new theoretical creation. Isaacs defines
    unconscious phantasy as mental reality:

> Psychic 'reality' (the reality of unconscious phantasy) is no less
> real than external reality. Isaacs offers here a brilliantly lucid
> explanation of the emphasis that Kleinians place on the reality
> of unconscious phantasy—it is not 'merely' or 'only' imagined,
> as something unreal, in contrast with what is actual.
>
> (Ogden, 2014, p. 931)

Here, too, Ogden is stressing one's capacity to hold together two
as-if opposing states of mind—fantasies are *real* and they do not
contradict one's ability to be connected to external reality, meaning that Ogden positions the unconscious phantasying within the
potential space or 'analytic third':

> To lose sight of either aspect of this set of dialectically con-
> stituted experiences of self and object – the experience of dif-
> ferentiated self and object and the experience of
> undifferentiated self and object – is to lose touch with the
> sophistication of Isaacs' thinking regarding forms of object-
> relating mediated by phantasy activity that occurs in the early
> mental life of the infant.
>
> (p. 935)

For Ogden, psychic development always entails the creation of a
wide range of ways that can 'bind together' subjective and objective realities. We need the external reality as brakes to our subjective experience, i.e., fantasies and unconscious fantasies:

> Psychological maturation, in general, and the development of
> the capacity for thinking, in particular, requires, for example,

that phantasies of omnipotent control over the breast and its supply of milk bump up against, and be modified by, the reality of hunger (which omnipotent phantasies cannot satisfy).

(p. 936)

Working with Unconscious Fantasies—Clinical Illustrations

In his paper "On potential space", Ogden (1985) gives a few clinical illustrations that I believe can help us understand his thinking in regard to the patient's unconscious fantasy, and to the importance of maintaining the dialectical tension between fantasy and reality.

> A borderline patient *knew* that the therapist, who had begun the hour three minutes late, did so because he preferred the patient whose hour preceded this patient's. The patient told the therapist that she had decided to terminate therapy, something she had been thinking about doing for a long time but had not previously told the therapist. Attempts on the part of the therapist to understand why the patient interpreted the lateness in this particular way were met with exasperation. The patient accused the therapist of relying on textbook interpretation to deny the obvious.
>
> (p. 134)

The patient Ogden describes is unable to refer to her 'fantasy' regarding the analyst's preference of the patient before her as an *emotional experience*. In fact, neither was she able to have any 'unconscious fantasies' concerning this distressing event—she had to turn it into something she *knew,* constructing it as a static (and dead) object (= a thought). Being certain about her perception made it impossible for her to do any *psychological work* with her distress, leading her to *act* upon it, instead of *experiencing* it. In this way, the patient eliminates the *potential space*, where new experiences can be generated and experienced. Lacking differentiation does not allow unconscious fantasies, or *phantasying,* to add colours and dimensions to the patient's immediate emotional experience. Not allowing any movement literally killed the therapy.

The second clinical illustration that Ogden presents (p. 135) is that of a young child who was allowed to witness his parents' intercourse and the labour of his younger sibling. The result of these traumatic experiences was that the child had developed a "precocious intelligence and a 'grownup' mode of relating that was marked by a profound scepticism" (p. 136). In a similar yet different manner to the previous patient this young child, too, lacked the capacity to bind together (unconscious) fantasy with a sense of reality. His reliance on 'reality,' using his as-if adult intelligence, was, in fact, his way to ward off unconscious fantasies. In other words, one could presume that the events this child was forced to witness were so overwhelming that he had to cut off his fantasies to protect himself.

In both cases, the patients experience *the collapse of the dialectical process between unconscious fantasy and external reality.* Such a collapse will often manifest itself by a lack of dreams or the dismissal of those they recall as 'senseless', 'crazy', 'stupid', 'weird', etc. Their dreams are often impossible to distinguish from their conscious thoughts, and they are usually preoccupied with detailing which parts of the dreams did, or did not, occur in reality.

Summary

Unconscious fantasy is a vital mechanism that contributes to our experience of *being alive.* It enriches our perception of both our internal and external reality; it colours all our experiences. What Ogden stresses most is the vital need for a dialectical process, the binding together of unconscious fantasy and our connection to reality. Pathology is often the result of the patient's inability (or reluctance) to hold on, simultaneously, to both. Under such circumstances, either the unconscious fantasy will overrule the patient's ability to connect to reality, or vice versa, the patient will (ab)use reality as a defence against fantasy. In either case, the patient's ability to *live fully* is damaged.

"Reading Winnicott"

Ogden's "Reading Winnicott" (2001) is one of many papers Ogden has written about Winnicott's theoretical thinking, specifically dedicated to Winnicott's "Primitive emotional development" (1945). Ogden's exploration of Winnicott's writing can be thought of as one's attempt of 'solving' a riddle—What is it that makes us feel most alive? And what does psychoanalysis have to do with it?

Ogden is *playing* with Winnicott's theory, much like a child plays with building blocks: The forms are there—square, round, triangular, and so are the colours. Yet, the child is invited to freely build endless objects, which will forever be the child's personal creation of what is presumably 'objective' and 'external' (a train, a house), yet these are objects whose qualities and possibilities are infinite, insofar as that specific child's imagination is infinite.

Ogden is fascinated not only by Winnicott's theoretical thinking but also by *the way Winnicott uses language as a personally created object*. Winnicott, perhaps more than any other psychoanalytic thinker, requires Ogden's interpretation, not only because reading Winnicott often feels like solving a mystery, but also because it requires one's ability to *play*. There are countless ways to read Winnicott, and Ogden invites his readers to experience Winnicott in his unique way, focusing on the issue of *aliveness* and *being:* What matters most is *how one lives one's life.*

It is not only Winnicott's theoretical thinking or clinical implementations that Ogden is fascinated with, but also Winnicott's *writing*. "Style and content are inseparable in writing", Ogden (2001) states (p. 300), and this is perhaps his most vital observation concerning Winnicott's writing, theory, and psychoanalytic practice. It is never solely *what* you say or do (i.e., content), but *how* (i.e., style). Ogden reads and teaches Winnicott in a Talmudic manner, line by line, aloud, as if the words need to be 'tasted' and 'sensed' by the reader. The reader is invited to *experience* the text, not merely *understand* it.

This is evident not only in Winnicott's often-concise writing but also in his psychoanalytic practice, which favours few (or no) interpretations. For Winnicott (and Ogden), words are 'objects', and their significance lies in *how one uses them*. Meaningful communication demands more than one's ability to *speak* words—it depends on *how* one uses words to facilitate *personal* meanings. Going back to Chomsky's theory of linguistic deep structures, I propose that whereas there is an inborn, biological-mental ability to acquire language, the capacity to use language in a meaningful way is a personal creation and a developmental achievement.

"Reading Winnicott" focuses on Winnicott's "Primitive emotional development" (1945), which Ogden considers to be Winnicott's "earliest major contribution to psychoanalysis" (Ogden, 2001, p. 300). Ogden's analysis can be equally applied to the psychoanalytic process in general; a process that allows patients to encounter their own 'text', i.e. their psychic-emotional contents, in a way that generates an imaginative experience through the medium of words and language. Psychoanalysis, like reading and writing, is an encounter between one's own 'self' and an 'other', meaning between one's internal world and the external reality. The following quote allows us to encounter Ogden-the-writer and Ogden-the-analyst:

> To speak of Winnicott's writing as literature is not to minimize its value as a way of conveying ideas that have proved to be of enormous importance to the development of psychoanalytic theory and practice; on the contrary, *my effort will be to demonstrate the ways in which the life of the writing is critical to, and inseparable from, the life of ideas.*
>
> (p. 300, italics added)

This passage encapsulates Ogden's perception of the intrinsic interconnection between form and content in Winnicott's work, emphasizing how *writing,* in its own right has the vitality that is crucial to, and inseparable from, the ideas it expresses. Ogden emphasizes the continuous nature of *writing* and *conveying* (the ideas), as indicated by the '-ing' endings. Writing and reading, as does psychoanalysis, is concerned with the dialectical discourse, of *self-discovery* and *self-expression.*

Living—Reading—Writing

For Ogden, writing is not merely a professional activity but the essence of *being alive.* It serves two purposes: (1) structuring thoughts internally; and (2) conveying ideas to the external world. Both are of (almost) equal importance, linking *internal and external realities.*

According to Ogden, Winnicott's writing has a 'voice' that is:

> Casual and conversational, yet always profoundly respectful of both the reader and the subject matter under discussion. The speaking voice gives itself permission to *wander*, and yet has the *compactness of poetry;* there is an *extraordinary intelligence* to the voice that is at the same time *genuinely humble* and *well aware of its limitations*; there is a *disarming intimacy* that at times *takes cover in wit* and *charm*; the voice is *playful* and *imaginative*, but *never folksy or sentimental* (italics added).
>
> (p. 301)

What a beautiful way to talk about the essence of psychoanalysis! Ogden magically *experiences* an *essence* of who Winnicott *is,* recreating psychoanalysis accordingly. Winnicott's papers are short but quite condensed. He tends to present his ideas as 'simple', often stopping in the middle of his paper, as if taking the reader 'aside', stating his main idea in a clear-cut way. Yet, his ideas are profoundly complex, particularly in their practical application; he is playful and serious, personal and formal, simple and complex, straight forward and paradoxical, and always creative. Being so creative means he gives no 'recipes' of how to conducts psychoanalysis; *'playing'* is, forever, a *'style'* that is personal and imaginative, meaning it is to be created, *anew*, each time.

This is how Ogden perceives psychoanalysis at its best—as an art, a continuous recreation:

> My own experience of rediscovering psychoanalysis involves three overlapping and interwoven variations: (1) *creating* psychoanalysis *freshly* in the process of *talking with* each patient in each analytic session; (2) *rediscovering* psychoanalysis in the experience of supervising and teaching psychoanalysis; and (3) "*dreaming up*" psychoanalysis for oneself in the act of *reading and writing* about analytic texts and literary works.
>
> (Ogden, 2009, p. 23, italics added)

This passage, quoted from Ogden's "Rediscovering Psychoanalysis" (2009) seems to sum up much of *how* Ogden practices psychoanalysis and what he values so much in Winnicott's thinking: (1) the analyst speaks *with* the patient (not *to* the patient); (2) psychoanalysis is a *creation* and should be *fresh* (not overloaded with over- saturated concepts and conceptualizations); (3) psychoanalysis requires that the analyst will be able to 'dream up' the patient; and (4) the experience entailed in reading and writing is another expression of the ability to 'dream' one's self into fuller existence.

Ogden (2011) quotes Winnicott, describing not only the healthy development of a baby, but also that of a patient, an analyst, and a writer:

> The individual's own *lived experience must be the basis for creating coherence for one's self and the integrity of oneself. Only after a sense of self has begun to come into being* (for the infant and for the writer) can one acknowledge the contributions of others to the creation one oneself (and one's ideas).
>
> (p. 302, italics added)

Conducting a good enough analysis demands that the analyst has already established a subjective self; this is required so the analyst can assist the patient to come into *being* (i.e., establish his or her own subjectivity). Only after *becoming a subject* can a baby, a patient, an analyst, or a writer acknowledge what they have been given by others. Prior to *being a subject*, it is impossible to acknowledge our dependency on others. *Becoming* a subject and *being* a subject is a continuous, *ongoing* process that should not be taken for granted. It is a psycho-developmental achievement, and one of the main 'goals' of Winnicott's aspired psychoanalytic endeavour.

Ogden stresses Winnicott's ability to create a 'new' psychoanalysis, parting from that of Freud and Klein. This is obvious in Winnicott's revision of their theory of depression:

> The depressed patient requires of his analyst the understanding that the analyst's work is to some extent his effort to cope with his own *(the analyst's)* depression, or shall I say guilt and grief resultant from the destructive elements in his own *(the analyst's love)*. To progress further along these lines,

the patient who is asking for help in regard to *his primitive, pre-depressive relationship to objects* needs his analyst to be able to see the analyst's undisplaced and coincidence love and hate of him.

> (Winnicott, 1945, p. 146–7, italics added)

This is a brilliant revision not only of Freud's and Klein's theoretical thinking about depression, but, in my opinion,—of their theoretical thinking about the *position of the analyst(!)* By referring twice to the analyst in brackets, Winnicott makes it very clear that he is talking about the *analyst's capabilities* and not those of the patient. It is the analyst who, first and foremost, has to be able to acknowledge his ambivalence towards the patient, meaning the analyst does not only 'love' the patient, but also 'hates' him. Winnicott's emphasis on the analyst's ambivalence, and his clear statement that he is talking about the *primitive, pre-depressive relationship to the object* is a declaration of what is needed, in the course of treating patients whose psychological make-up is emotionally primitive, and what is *different* from what Freud and Klein suggested. Winnicott does not specify what the patient actually needs from the analyst in such cases. However, I think much of what is needed is described in the previous passage, i.e., (1) the analyst's ability to *live an experience together with the patient; (2)* the analyst's ability to *talk with the patient* and *not to the patient;* (3) the analyst's ability for *being;* and (4) for being *playful;* and, perhaps more than anything else, (5) the analyst's ability to rediscover, and recreate, psychoanalysis anew with each patient.

Another important idea implicit in Winnicott's revolutionary theoretical construction of depression refers to the function and significance of the analytic setting ('frame'):

> Viewing it as a *medium for the expression of the analyst's hatred of the patient* ... These words derive a good deal of their power from the fact that the truth of the idea that the analyst expresses his hate in these actions (which are so ordinary as to frequently go unnoticed) is immediately recognizable by the analytic reader as part of his experience with virtually every patient.

> (Ogden, 2001, p. 305)

Ogden puts forward Winnicott's ability to normalize something that analysts (and therapists) may find difficult to admit—we do not only 'love' our patients, we also 'hate' them. Winnicott's matter-of-fact tone of voice makes it easier not only to admit this, but also to see it as human and forgivable. I draw a direct line between this normalizing of emotions that may be difficult to own and the profound significance that Winnicott attributes to the *true self.* Not owning our hate hinders our ability to love. Being 'real' and living fully requires us to own (and re-own) as many aspects of ourselves (emotions, fantasies, thoughts, etc.) as possible. When we deny parts of who we really are, we kill off significant parts of ourselves.

In presenting one of (the few available) Winnicott's clinical illustrations, Ogden (p. 307) stresses Winnicott's subtle way of presenting the reader with his revision of the analytic technique:

> Winnicott then provides the reader with a *major revision of analytic technique. He accomplishes this so subtly that the reader is apt not to notice it if he is not attending carefully to what is going in the writing.* Nothing short of a new way of *being with* and *talking to patients* is *being offered* to the reader, *without preaching or fanfare: 'sometimes we must interpret this [the patient's giving every detail of his week-end] as the patient's need to be known in all his bits and pieces by one person,* the analyst'.

> (p. 308, italics added)

This passage draws a parallel between Winnicott's theory of good enough maternal care of the infant and the analyst's care for the patient: (1) the analyst's interventions should be so *subtle* that the patient hardly notices them; (2) the analyst's best intervention is *being with the patient;* (3) this is specifically significant with patients whose emotional development is still 'primitive', that is patients who are not yet able to be *talked with,* but must be *talked to* (you *talk to* a baby before it has become a subject); (4) interpretations should be *offered* to the patient, not *preached;* and, lastly, (5) when in such a delicate state (describing the weekends in great detail), the patient may need to experience the gathering of all his 'bits and pieces' into one person—the analyst.

Clinical Illustrations

The following clinical illustration is taken from Ogden's paper "Fear of breakdown and the unlived life" (2014). Ogden's patient, Ms. L, who was in a four-sessions-a-week analysis, tended to repeatedly "fall in love with men who seemed to her to return her love" (p. 216). The specific incidence that Ogden discusses is Ms. L's crush on an occasional salesman, with whom she spoke for barely a few moments. That did not prevent her from feeling extremely disappointed and humiliated when she realized that he "dropped her" to talk "with just anybody who walked through the front door of the showroom" (p. 216). For the next two weeks, Ms. L parked her car, every single day, across the showroom, watching the salesman—"during the months that followed, the patient could think of little other than how much she longed for this man" (p. 216).

For a while Ogden talked with (or to) the patient about the possible similarities of her feeling of being "dropped" by the salesman to her feelings towards him, following the inevitable endings of each session, the weekends and his occasional vacations. Ms. L opposed all these interpretations, and eventually Ogden "put a stop to the way I [he] was talking to her" (p. 217). Ogden then attempted to "let his mind 'go loose', using reveries to sense something new. Alas, soon enough afterwards, this, too, felt to him as yet "another prefabricated analytic technique" (p. 217). It took him time to real-ize that "what was most *real* about what was occurring between Ms. L and me [him] was the experience of sterility on both our parts" (p. 217). Ogden then intervenes in a way that I perceive to be courageous, telling the patient that he came to believe that "whatever it is about you that makes you persist in tracking those men is the healthiest part of you" (p. 217). Naturally, the patient was surprised, asking him whether he was making fun of her. Ogden was, of course, not making fun of her—he had just real-ized something crucial about this patient: As an unloved and uncared for child, she was so lonely that she had created, for herself, a world of imaginary objects. Yet this was not an adequate substitute for *real* people and *real relationships*. Her persistent tracking of possible love objects, however 'bizarre' it may have seemed at first, was, in fact, her dedication to finding what she was missing and been longing for her entire life. Following this *new real-ization*, Ms. L was able to offer Ogden a genuine piece of herself, saying: "I've had the impression for some time now that you've given up on me, that you're continuing to meet with me only because you don't know how to get out of this" (p. 218).

This was, in fact, what Ogden was able to *sense,* at last—that the patient's persistence was that part of her that *had not given up,* on herself, her emotional needs and her dreams. The patient was 'obsessed' with men that did not care for her or not even acknowledged her existence, but they were, at least, *'real'* men, and not imaginary ones. This realization of Ogden allowed the two of them to find new ways to talk about the patient's *real* feelings of longing and shame, pain and fear, and of her unreluctant search for *being* and *feeling* alive.

On Living as Dreaming, and Vice Versa

The idea that 'dreaming' and 'being and feeling alive' are mutually interdependent is central to Ogden's theoretical thinking and writing. In what follows, I will discuss some of Ogden's theoretical and clinical contributions, focusing on his two papers "On not being able to dream" (2003) and "On holding and containing, being and dreaming" (2004d).

I perceive Ogden's paper "On not being able to dream" as an elaboration of his re-contextualization of Winnicott's and Bion's thinking as ontological. Ogden has written several papers on dreaming, in a way that bridges Winnicott's and Bion's thinking, offering his own theoretical thinking about the profound role dreaming plays in facilitating the patients' *sense of aliveness.*

> Bion (1962c) introduced the term 'alpha-function' to refer to the as yet unknown set of mental operations that, together, transform raw sense impressions ('beta-elements') into elements of experience (termed 'alpha elements') which can be stored as unconscious memory in a form that makes them accessible for *creating linkages necessary for unconscious as well as pre-conscious and conscious psychological work,* such as *dreaming, thinking, repressing, remembering, forgetting, mourning, reverie and learning from experience.*
>
> (Ogden, 2003, p. 17–18, italics added)

Ogden perceives dreaming as a *form of psychological work* carried out at all levels of consciousness: conscious, preconscious, and unconscious. The psychological work facilitated by dreaming is supported by other mental functions such as thinking, repressing, remembering, forgetting, mourning, reverie, and learning from experience. These functions are composed of (or begin with) beta-elements—various raw sense impressions, which Ogden refers to as '*noises*'. These 'noises' (impressions) are *meaningless unless the 'alpha-function' is utilized*. Without the structuring that the 'alpha-function' allows, these primitive sensual impressions are nothing but 'noise' which can be "very roughly compared with 'snow' on a malfunctioning television screen in which no single visual scintillation or group of scintillations can be linked with other scintillations to form an image or even a meaningful pattern" (p. 18).

Ogden integrates into his theory of dreaming (and of not being able to dream) Bion's idea that dreaming is not (and should not be) limited to being asleep, but can take place during sleep and awake states; being, essentially, *an emotional experience*. The utilization of the alpha-function is necessary for both the ability to dream and the ability to be awake: "[In as much as] alpha-function makes the [raw] sense impressions of the emotional experience available for conscious [thought] and dream-thought, the patient who cannot dream cannot go to sleep and cannot wake up" (Bion, 1962c, p. 7/ Ogden, 2003, p. 18).

The idea that *dreaming* serves the same psycho-mental function, whether we are asleep or awake, is revolutionary and bears significant implications for psychoanalytic work, particularly for the role the analyst's reveries have in terms of the experience of transference and countertransference. If a patient cannot use the 'alpha-function' (the analyst's or his/her own), the raw sense impressions (i.e., 'beta-elements') remain *untransformed*. In such cases, the patient cannot differentiate between being asleep and being awake, meaning he/she is *unable to engage in any psychological work*. A common manifestation of this condition is a patient who cannot distinguish between internal reality and external reality, or between sensations, feelings, and actions. If a patient cannot dream (or cannot differentiate internal from external reality), his psychological growth is hindered. Dreaming is a process of performing unconscious psychological work, relying on the ability to link together elements of experience:

> This work of *making unconscious linkages*—as *opposed to forms of psychic evacuation, such as hallucination, excessive projective identification, manic defence, and paranoid delusion*—allows one unconsciously and consciously to think about and make psychological use of experience. *A person unable to learn from (make use of) experience is imprisoned in the hell of an endless, unchanging world of what is.*
>
> (p. 19, italics added)

'Linking' and 'evacuation' are fundamentally different, perhaps even opposing, forms of communication. Analytic work refers only to the type of psychological work and communication that involves linking. Ogden argues that this distinction can be applied to various psycho-mental conditions, such as hallucinations, learning, and dreaming. Linking is the only means by which we can learn, change, and make progress. When linking is not possible, there can be no change, and the patient becomes trapped in a motionless state, which can evolve into a 'deadened' existence.

Bion's expansion of the role of dreams, from "constructing narratives (with manifest and latent meanings)" (p. 19), aligns with Ogden's ontological theory and the role he attributes to psychoanalysis: "Bion, in this passage, reverses the conventional wisdom that the ability to fall asleep is a precondition for dreaming. He proposes instead that dreaming is what makes it possible to fall asleep and to wake up" (p. 19).

For Ogden, psychoanalysis is not about receiving answers or understanding; it is about asking questions and dreaming oneself into fuller existence. It is about gaining a conscious existence and being awake: "The term '*being asleep*' becomes, in Bion's hands, a conception of being '*unconscious of certain elements* [the repressed] that cannot penetrate the barrier presented by his 'dream'" (p. 15, italics added).

Similarly, "being awake now signifies being uninterruptedly conscious of what is going on in waking life (for example, listening to a patient, reading a book, or viewing a film)" (p. 19).

Psychoanalysis is a state of mind, not necessarily confined to therapy or the consulting room.

A 'psychoanalytic experience' can occur when we visit a museum, listen to music, write, or take a walk in the wilderness. It is about being awake and conscious of what is happening, both internally and externally: *"Dreaming, from this vantage point, is what allows us to create and maintain the structure of our mind,* organized around the differentiation of, and the *mediated conversation* between, our conscious life and our unconscious life" (p. 20, italics added).

This ability to differentiate between the conscious and unconscious, between 'being awake' and 'being asleep,' is a vital component of mental health and marks the difference between 'being alive' and not: "The differentiation of, and interplay between, conscious and *unconscious life is created by—not simply reflected in—*dreaming. In this important sense, *dreaming makes us human"* (p. 20, italics added).

Ogden 'borrows' Bion's conceptual idea of 'not being able to dream':

> It used to be said that a man had a nightmare because he had indigestion, and that is why he woke up in a panic. *My version is: The sleeping patient is panicked because he cannot have a nightmare; he cannot wake up or go to sleep;* he has had mental indigestion ever since.
>
> (Bion, 1962a, p. 8/Ogden, 2003, p. 20, italics added)

If a person cannot dream and not even have a nightmare, he may not be able to distinguish between being awake (conscious and *alive*) and being asleep (unconscious and mentally and emotionally *dead*). Ogden (2004a) draws a parallel between Winnicott ('holding' and 'being') and Bion ('containing' and 'dreaming'), distinguishing between the two:

> I believe that the confusion regarding the concepts of *'holding"* and the *'container–contained'* derives, to a considerable degree, from Bion's penchant for using words in a way that invents them anew. In Bion's hands, the word *'container'*— with its benign connotations of a stable, sturdy delineating

function—*becomes a word that denotes the full spectrum of ways of processing experience,* from the most destructive and deadening to the most creative and growth-promoting."

(p. 1349, italics added)

Ogden argues that Bion's container is *not* a static act, but does possess epistemological quality, as its main concern is with 'knowing' and 'understanding'. Winnicott's concept of 'holding', a complex conceptualization of a *process,* that profoundly impacts the baby's emotional growth has an ontological quality to it, as its focus is on *experience* and *experiencing*:

The importance of the impact of maternal holding on the emotional growth of the infant would be disputed by very few psychoanalysts. However, the significance to psychoanalytic theory of Winnicott's concept of holding is far more subtle than this broad statement would suggest. Holding, for Winnicott, is an *ontological concept* that he uses to explore the *specific qualities of the experience of being alive* at different developmental stages, as well *as the changing intrapsychic–interpersonal means by which the sense of continuity of being is sustained over time.*

(p. 1350, italics added)

Ogden's differentiation between 'containing' and 'holding' refers to the dialectical tension between epistemological and ontological psychoanalysis. Although in 2019 he grouped Winnicott and Bion together as 'ontological,' in the earlier paper (Ogden, 2004a) he perceives them as two different conceptual processes, allowing *different modes of facilitation of mental and emotional growth of the baby.* One significant difference between the two concepts has to do with the 'motion' within the baby-mother (patient-analyst) unit. In 'holding', it is the mother-analyst who join the baby, safeguarding the baby's state of 'going-on-being'. This important ability of the mother-analyst is most needed at the earliest phases of the baby's emotional development, when the baby-patient do not, yet, have a *subjectivity* of their own and it is the mother-analyst who must hold this for them. Ogden (2004a) relates to it as the mother's-analyst's ability *'to be in the infant's (patient's) time'.*

'Holding'—Clinical Illustration

Ogden (2004d, p. 1351) presents a clinical illustration of Ms. R, a mother of two adolescents, who has lost her own mother six months earlier. In the vignette Ogden describes the patient's 'over sensitivity' to everything the analyst says or does. Everything seems to bother the patient, even the analyst's breathing, moving, etc. It seemed that the patient was unable to be aware of any aspect of the environment. Ogden's reverie took him back to the nights he spent sitting by his son's bed, waiting for him to fall asleep. He then recalled how, when his son finally fell asleep, his breathing began matching his son's, as if they unified. In one of these half-asleep hours of waiting for his son to fall asleep, Ogden had a dream, in which his wife and sons had suddenly disappeared. Being at one with his son allowed him to not only breathe together, but also to possibly dream his son's deepest fears. Ogden used this reverie as a way of *experiencing* what his patient was feeling and of her need—she needed him to *be* with her, to *join her own (psychic) time*, which is completely internal and healthily ignorant of *external time and objects*.

Container–Contained

As far as Ogden is concerned, "the idea of the container–contained addresses not *what* we think, but the *way* we think, that is, how we process lived experience and what occurs psychically when we are unable to do psychological work with that experience" (p. 1354).

Ogden awards attention to an idea that rarely receives one, that is that the 'container–contained' is, in fact "the psycho-analytic *function of the personality*" (p. 1355, italics added). Similarly perhaps to Chomsky's 'deep structure', or Klein's and Isaacs' 'unconscious fantasy', Ogden suggests that in Bion's perception, "the human personality is constitutionally equipped with the potential for a set of mental operations that serves the function of doing conscious and unconscious psychological work on emotional experience (a process that issues in psychic growth)" (p. 1355).

By referring to these mental operations as 'psychoanalytic,' Bion is also defining what psychoanalysis is about, "that is, the viewing of experience simultaneously from the vantage points of the conscious and unconscious mind" (p. 1355).

This, Ogden connects to the operation of dreaming: "Dreaming involves *a form* of psychological work in which there takes place *a generative conversation between preconscious aspects of the mind and disturbing thoughts, feelings and fantasies* that are precluded from, yet pressing towards conscious awareness (the dynamic unconscious)" (p. 1355, italics added).

Besides 'dreams' and 'dreaming', there is also the idea of 'dream thoughts'. As I mentioned before, for Bion (and Ogden), dreaming occurs while asleep, or awake. Bion's conceptualization of dreaming and its functional role is opposite to that of Freud. For Bion, dreams and dreaming do not function as a disguise for unwanted, or unbearable sensations, feelings or thoughts. Rather, "Bion's work of dreaming is that set of mental operations that allows conscious lived experience to be altered in such a way that it becomes available to the unconscious for psychological work (dreaming)" (p. 1356).

In this sense, 'dreams', 'dreaming', 'dream thoughts' and 'container–contained', all function as means of feeling, or *being* more *alive*. Psychic growth occurs when the 'container' (i.e., the ability for dreaming, whether asleep or awake) has a good 'relationship' with the 'contained' (i.e., one's unconscious thoughts that result from emotional experiences that one experiences as being *alive*). A crucial aspect of this process is that it has to benefit both parties, 'container' and 'contained,' allowing both of them to grow, psychologically. Psychological growth expresses itself in different ways—a patient may start to dream, or be able to remember his/her dreams, or be willing to 'think' about the dream. Being able to experience more emotions in a deeper way, etc.— represents one's psychological growth.

'Container–Contained'—Clinical Illustration

Ogden presents a vignette describing his way of working with 'container–contained' (p. 1359).

Ms. N began each of her analytic sessions with telling Ogden, in great detail, everything that had happened to her the day before, specifically how she had managed to make good use of some insight that came up in that day's session. She would then pause, waiting for him to praise her progress. This caused Ogden to feel angry, as if the patient was simply assigning him a 'role' in a script that she had written. "'Scripting' and feeding me my 'lines' were metaphors that Ms N and I had developed to refer to her *efforts to expunge her awareness of the separateness of our minds and our lives*" (p. 1360, italics added). This was also connected by the patient and Ogden to her childhood experiences of feeling that her mother was referring to her as if the two of them were one another's extensions.

Ms. N developed various ways of attending to her feelings of emptiness (e.g., engaging saleswomen in expensive clothing stores, trying on endless looks, having them tell her, maternally, how pretty she looked, p. 1360). On the eighth year of her analysis, the patient brought in a dream, to which Ogden's first reaction was as before, meaning that he felt as if the patient was 'manipulating' him into a specific emotional reaction.

> But there was something subtly different about the dream and the way the patient told it to me. It felt to me that, in the middle of a compulsive repetition of an all too familiar pattern of relatedness, something else obtruded when Ms N described the earrings. Her voice became less sing-song in tone and her speech slowed as if gently placing the two tiny eggs in the bird's nest.
>
> (p. 1360)

Listening to the patient's dream is listening not only to *what* she says, but to *how* she says it. It is like listening to a song—the music is an experience equal to the lyrics (Ogden, 2018b). While listening to the dream, what enabled a turning point in Ogden's *experience* were the nuances, the patient's tone of voice, the change in the rhythm of her speaking, etc. Ms. N ended her telling of the dream by saying "I managed to get out of the store without buying anything!" giving Ogden the feeling that her victory was the feeling that she had full control over the analytic session. This thought led to a reverie

> of having gone shopping with my closest friend, J, a few years after we had graduated from college. The two of us were looking for an engagement ring for him to give to the woman with whom he was living. Neither of us knew the first thing about diamonds—or any other kind of jewellery. *This shopping experience was one filled with feelings of warmth and closeness*, but at the same time I was aware that there was a way in which I was participating in an event (the process of J's getting married) that I feared would change (or maybe even bring to an end) the friendship as it had existed to that point.
> (pp. 1360–1)

Following the reverie, Ogden asked the patient why she hadn't bought the earrings that she found so beautiful. This was an unexpected analytic question, as it referred to the dream as if it was a 'real' event. Ogden was also surprised to realize that his emotional reaction was unusually not angry. To his surprise, the patient paused for a moment (again, an unusual reaction on her behalf) and then replied, as if the dream was indeed an 'actual event': "I don't know. The idea never occurred to me" (p. 1361). Ogden understands this dream as a representation of the patient's inability to make use of the function of the 'container–contained'. It was obvious from the way she could not use anything Ogden had given to her in the sessions, which was represented in the dream by a "tinny (inhuman) voice from the mechanical speaker system" (p. 1361).

It was Ogden's own dream (i.e., reverie) that served as a new 'container' for what were his feelings of hostility towards the patient. He needed his own experience of going shopping with his best friend, an event that was full of warmth and affection, and the sudden change of the emotional climate, realizing he was also jealous and worried about the possibility of losing his friend following the friend's marriage, to be able to feel differently about the patient. Ogden's reverie was his way of joining the patient's dream; he was, in fact, dreaming the dream that she was still unable to dream on her own.

Understanding Versus Experiencing

In the paper 'Intuiting the truth of what's happening: On Bion's "Notes on memory and desire", Ogden (2015) analyses one of Bion's most famous works, in an attempt to sort out the foundations of the analytic process: What is it that is most helpful and important in facilitating the patient's psychological growth? Ogden's answer, as it seems to me, lies in the paper's title: 'truth' and 'intuition' are especially important.

Ogden puzzles the reader by stating that it took him decades to grapple with Bion's "impossible" paper, which is "only two and a half pages in length" (p. 285). He begins his paper with a recurring assertion from his writings:

> An individual's ideas are only as valuable as the use to which they are put by others. It has taken me thirty years of studying Bion's 'Notes on Memory and Desire' (1967) to be able to put into words something of what I have made with this paper.
>
> (p. 285)

For me, several key ideas emerge from these opening lines:

1   An idea is an 'object', and its vitality comes only through its use. This recalls Winnicott's (1969) concept of 'the use of the object'. The ability to use someone else's ideas is an achievement that often requires time and effort to transform this 'object' into one's own creation.
2   It often takes a long time to develop this ability to creatively engage with the ideas of others. Readers are immediately drawn to the question: What is it about this short paper that makes it so challenging to 'put into words'?

Why did it take Ogden three decades to articulate his understanding? The answer is only partially revealed in the following ontological reflection:

> It is only recently that I have recognized that my effort to *understand* the paper is misplaced. It is a paper that *asks not*

to be understood. It asks of the reader something more difficult than *understanding* and promises the reader something
more valuable than *understanding*.

(Ogden, 2015, p. 286, italics added)

Ogden's *ontological perspective* becomes clearer as the word
'understanding' appears four times in this passage, *consistently in
a negative context*. He ensures that we, the readers, grasp his
message: The famous recommendation of 'no memory and no
desire', which generations of analysts (including Ogden himself,
over the past thirty years) have attempted to understand, *is not
meant to be understood. Nor is it about understanding at all.*

So, what is it about? In the next paragraph, Ogden provides
what seems to be a straightforward answer:

It is about *intuitive thinking*, and the ways in which *intuitive
thinking* works in the analytic situation; it is about the fact
that we cannot be taught how to interpret what we *sense*
concerning the patient's unconscious psychic truths. Nor can
we be taught how to convey to the patient that we have
intuited those truths, much less what it is that we have *intuited*;
nor can we be taught whether it is wise to convey now, or
perhaps tomorrow, something of what we *sense* about the
patient's unconscious psychic reality, or whether it might be
best never to convey what we *sense* concerning those truths
that the patient holds most sacred.

(p. 286, italics added)

Two key words are repeated: 'intuitive' (or 'intuitive thinking') and
'sense'. Both concepts are relatively vague, and Ogden insists that
they cannot be taught. The mystery, therefore, remains unre-
solved. How can an analyst as skilled and rational as Ogden
advocate for a psychoanalysis that is rooted in intuition and sensory perception—concepts that defy teaching? To put it cheekily,
one might say that, intuitively speaking, this does not make sense.
It seems that in the following paragraph, Ogden digresses slightly
to articulate another recurring idea of his, regarding the analytic
reader's task:

> I am trying to write 'Memory and Desire' as my own paper,
> not in the *sense* of passing off as mine what is Bion's, but in
> the *sense* of writing the paper as a paper that reflects the ways
> I have been changed by Bion's paper, as opposed to what I
> have learned from it.
>
> (p. 286, italics added)

Ogden has expressed this idea many times across his works. This
repetition is neither forgetfulness nor redundancy, but an intentional
transmission of an essential concept: Bion's ideas matter only insofar
as they can be 'sensed' by others. Ogden's reading of this paper is
personal. He is not attempting to write the 'truth' about Bion's theoretical ideas; he is presenting his own personal truth of the way he
has 'made sense' of Bion's thinking. For Ogden, psychoanalysis is a
deeply personal psycho-emotional *experience* and even more so—it
is about *experiencing*. What makes an idea 'true' is its capacity to
foster an experience, learning and change within the patient and the
analyst. In some sense, if an 'idea' cannot be 'used' by others, in their
own unique way, it amounts to a 'dead' object, devoid of meaning
and significance. Interestingly, Ogden regards Bion's (1967) paper as
'an unfinished paper' (a paper that has not 'died'): "A *sketch,* the
beginnings of lines of thought of a sort *that do not lend themselves to
being completed,* but that invite both elaboration and response"
(Ogden, 2015, p. 287, italics added).

I believe Ogden's view of Bion's paper reflects his broader perspective on psychoanalysis: psychic growth is an unfinished process, and each idea or experience that arises, in a session, is
fundamentally a 'sketch', never fully completed. Writing, reading,
practicing psychoanalysis—and perhaps life itself—are invitations
for 'collaborations' and joint effort, requiring the participation of
at least two people.

Discussing Bion's (1967) paper, Ogden states that "the significance of this paper lies not in its dictate to 'cultivate a watchful
avoidance of memory' (Bion 1967, p. 137) and to desist from
'desires for results, cure, or even understanding'".

> To my mind, it proposes a revised analytic methodology.
> 'Bion supplants "*awareness*" from its central role in the

analytic process and, in its place, instates the analyst's (largely unconscious) work of *intuiting* the psychic reality (the truth) of the session by becoming at one with it.

(Ogden, 2015, p. 287, italics added)

For Ogden, Bion's primary contribution is the *shift from a traditional epistemological approach to psychoanalysis toward a practice rooted in ontology.* Bion is offering a revised analytic methodology, one grounded in the analyst's capacity to *intuit the psychic reality* (or 'truth') of whatever is unfolding in the session. This is achieved by the analyst becoming at one with the session itself. Ogden is careful not to claim ownership of 'understanding' Bion's intentions. Rather, he presents his *personal application of those ideas.* In doing so, Ogden exemplifies what he means by re-creating an existing text as a collaborative endeavour; his theoretical approach is characterized by questioning rather than providing definitive answers.

Both Ogden the 'reader' and Ogden the 'analyst' use a method that relies on 'impressions': "I shift to a method of reading in which I allow unanswered questions to accrue until I begin to form *impressions* (as opposed to *understandings*)—impressions that suggest, but *only suggest, meaning*' (p. 288, italics added).

Ogden's attention lingers on Bion's use of the term 'sense impressions', which references Freud's paper, "Formulations on the two principles of mental functioning" (1911). Bion has, throughout his career, developed a psychoanalytic theory of thinking, modifying, and sometimes rejecting Freud's ideas. One idea they both emphasized was the centrality of *reality* to one's *thinking.*

For Ogden, reality is synonymous with truth. He goes even further, suggesting that: "In the spirit of Bion's paper, I would rename the reality principle and the pleasure principle *the truth-seeking principle* and *the truth-fearing principle,* respectively" (Ogden, 2015, p. 289, italics in original).

Ogden's interpretation of Freud's 'pleasure principle' is that it is a defence against 'reality' and 'truth', yet it raises at least two questions: (1) What does this concept suggest about 'dreaming' and the 'unconscious'? And (2) What does it mean to speak of 'truth' within psychoanalysis? Ogden's response to these questions is as follows:

"I would paraphrase this in the following way: memory and desire "exercise and intensify" those mental operations that have their origins in the response of the organism to sensory stimuli. Memory and desire enhance the power of the sense organs, which are "designed to serve [conscious] impressions of sense" and the power of the pleasure (truth-fearing) principle. *In so doing, memory and desire undermine genuine unconscious thinking (and thereby contribute to "absence of mind").*

(p. 289, italics added)

Many ask themselves the next questions: (1) How can an analyst who cares about their patients not remember past sessions (or anything else, for that matter,) or be without desire? And (2) Should we not have the desire to help our patients and remember what we have discussed?

As far as Ogden is concerned, 'memory' and 'desire' distance us from the 'here and now', that is, from what is 'really' happening in the session. 'Memory' takes us back to the past, and 'desire' propels us into the future. In that sense, memory and desire distance us from the truth and hinder our ability for thinking:

In my rewriting of 'Memory and Desire,' I would like to make explicit what I believe to be implicit in the paragraph under discussion: *genuine thinking, which is predominantly unconscious, seeks out the truth (reality).* This, I believe, is the core of Bion's theory of thinking. Moreover, *sensory experience distracts from and undermines genuine thinking.* Without the truth (O3), or at least openness to it, thinking is not only impossible; the very idea of thinking becomes meaningless, just as the readings of a compass are rendered meaningless in the absence of a North Pole.

(p. 290, italics in original)

Being attuned to the 'here and now' of the session allows the analyst's 'dreaming' (having reveries), 'experiencing', and 'thinking': "Psychoanalytic *'observation'* is concerned neither with what has happened nor with what is going to happen but with what is happening" (Bion 1967, p. 136, italics in original).

Another of Bion's ideas that Ogden seeks to elucidate is the idea of 'intuition' and 'intuiting':

Furthermore, *it [analytic "observation"] is not concerned with sense impressions or objects of sense.* Any psychoanalyst knows depression, anxiety, fear and other aspects of psychic reality whether those aspects have been or can be successfully named or not. Of its reality he has no doubt. Yet anxiety, to take one example, has no shape, no smell, no taste.

(Bion 1967, p. 136/Ogden, 2015, p. 291, italics added)

Concerning Bion's statement that the psychoanalyst's 'real world' consists of "depression, anxiety, fear and other aspects of psychic reality" (Bion 1967, p. 136), Ogden suggests that Bion is primarily concerned with differentiating between conscious and unconscious realities:

The realm of the unconscious, Bion vehemently insists, is the realm of the psychoanalyst—*no one knows the unconscious in the way that the psychoanalyst does, and he must protect it from being "confounded"* (Bion 1967, p. 137) *with the conscious realm of experience.* The unconscious is the realm of thinking and feeling that together form the psychic reality (psychoanalytic truth) of an individual at any given moment.

(Ogden, 2015, p. 292, italics added)

This paragraph introduces an intriguing idea, as complex as the previous: *the analyst's experience belongs to the conscious realm, while thinking and feeling constitute the unconscious realm.* At this point, Ogden delves into the concept of 'intuition'—a somewhat nebulous term in general and even more so in the context of psychoanalysis. The first idea Bion addresses is the analyst's awareness, particularly the 'evenly floating attention' that is widely regarded as crucial: "Awareness of the sensuous accompaniments of emotional experience are [sic] a hindrance to the psychoanalyst's intuition of the reality with which he must be at one"

(Bion 1967, p. 136/Ogden, 2015, p. 292, italics in original)

Ogden elaborates:

> It is widely accepted that the analyst is interested in the 'sensuous accompaniments' of his visual awareness of such events as the patient's gait as she walks to the couch, olfactory awareness of the scent of perfume or perspiration in the consulting room, the auditory awareness of music or cacophony or drone of the patient's voice, and so on.
>
> > (p. 292)

Ogden argues that the closing of Bion's paragraph captures the essence of his revolutionary idea: the "sensuous accompaniments of emotional experience [that] are a hindrance to 'the psychoanalyst's intuition of the reality with which he must be at one'" (Bion 1967, p. 136, emphasis added/Ogden, 2015, p. 293).

If the analyst wishes "to be genuinely analytic in the way he observes," they "must rely on a wholly different form of perceiving and thinking" (p. 293):

> That form of thinking, which Bion calls *intuition*, has its roots in the unconscious mind. *Receptivity to sense impressions, "awareness", and "understanding" are the domain of conscious thought processes.* For Bion (1962a), unconscious thinking is far richer than conscious (predominantly secondary process) thinking, which is required to conduct the business of waking life. The unconscious is free to view experience simultaneously from multiple vertices, which would create havoc if one were to use such thinking while trying to carry out the tasks and conduct the interpersonal relationships of waking life.
>
> > (Ogden, 2015, p. 293, italics added)

Ogden draws on Bion's ideas to develop his ontological perspective on the psychoanalyst's primary task: "[It] is not that of *understanding* or *figuring out* the nature of the psychic reality of the moment in the analytic session; rather, *the analyst's work is to intuit that unconscious psychic reality* by becoming at one with it" (pp. 293–4, italics added).

Ogden links intuition to dreaming:

> When we dream—both when we are asleep and when we are awake (Bion 1962a)—we have the experience of sensing (intuiting) the reality of an aspect of our unconscious life, and we are at one with it. Dreaming, in the way I am using the term, is a transitive verb. In dreaming, we are not dreaming about something; we are dreaming something, 'dreaming up' an aspect of ourselves. In dreaming, we are at one with the reality of the dream; we are the dream. While dreaming, we are intuiting (dreaming up) *an element of our unconscious emotional lives and are at one with it in a way that differs from any other experience.* In dreaming, we are most real to ourselves; we are most ourselves.
>
> (Ogden, 2015, p. 294, italics added)

In this passage, Ogden invites us, the readers, into his vision of what dreaming is fundamentally about. It is *an experience*, and *the experiencing* of some aspect of our 'selves,' and of something that 'is happening' to us, that needs our *being*; it is 'something' that is *vital* for who we 'really' are, without which our lives will be not as 'whole' or 'complete'. Our dreams enable us to 're-own' some lost aspect of ourselves.

Dreaming, and the ability to dream, is among the most precious gifts psychoanalysis offers to both analyst and patient:

> For me, *reverie* (Bion 1962a,1962b; Ogden 1997c), *waking dreaming, is paradigmatic of the clinical experience of intuiting the psychic reality of a moment of an analysis.* In order to enter *a state of reverie*, which in the analytic setting *is always in part an intersubjective phenomenon* (Ogden 1994), *the analyst must engage in an act of self-renunciation.* By self-renunciation, I mean t*he act of allowing oneself to become less definitively oneself in order to create a psychological space in which analyst and patient may enter into a shared state of intuiting and being-atone- with a disturbing psychic reality that the patient, on his own, is unable to bear.*
>
> (Ogden, 2015, p. 294, italics added)

In this single paragraph, Ogden condenses what he sees as the analyst's two most essential tools in clinical work:

1 Reverie
2 The analytic third

These two states of mind are interconnected. For the analyst to experience reverie, they must be able to "become less definitively oneself". This creates a new, intermediate space that facilitates the 'analytic thirdness'—a shared psychological realm where analyst and patient can both be, and not be, simultaneously creating something new. Patient and analyst create psychoanalysis together and they are both transformed by it: *"The analyst and the patient have already been changed by the experience of jointly intuiting the unsettling psychic reality with which they have been at one"* (p. 296, italics in original).

Clinical Illustration

The following clinical illustration is from Ogden (2015):

Ms. C was in a five-sessions-a-week analysis for several years, when Ogden began feeling that, upon meeting her in the waiting room, the patient was (as if) in the wrong place. The feeling of 'strangeness' was such that Ogden had the urge to tell her that she *was* in the wrong place and that the person she had come to see in another building near by. On the occasion that Ogden describes, once the patient lied down on the couch, he felt an impulse to say "I love you" (p. 297).

Soon after, the patient told him a dream she had the previous night, in which she had lost something, not knowing what it was. Ogden's response to this is perhaps the most astonishing one I have ever heard of. He asked her: "Is loving me such a terrible thing that you have to leave it somewhere else when you come to see me?" (p. 297).

The patient's response to this, is not any less astonishing and courageous. She said: "You've never told me that you love me before." To which Ogden replied: "Would my love be in the wrong place if I were to love you?" And the patient said: "Yes, I think it would, but I would feel empty if I were to give it back."

The rest of their conversation moves, back and forth, on the edge between 'fantasy' and 'facts', or 'reality' (when the patient tells Ogden she loves him but that could not be 'real' because he is her analyst and not a 'real' man she could date or marry). Ogden concludes this part of their conversation by saying to Ms. C:

> "When you tell me about 'facts that can't be undone', I feel as if you're killing something or someone. You kill the person you love by saying I don't exist, and by saying I'm no one, so it's a waste of life to give me the love that you feel." I paused, and then said, "I think that in one way you'd like to hear me say, 'You and your love are in the right place. This is exactly the place for them.' But in another way, it would be terribly frightening if I were to say that."
>
> (p. 298)

In my experience this conversation is Ogden's invitation for dreaming—on the edge between (external) 'reality,' in which he and patient should not fall in love, and 'fantasy,' (meaning 'internal reality'), in which they *can* love one another, experiencing this love as being 'in the right place'. Such a dream can elicit different feelings, including fear, but *not being able to dream it, means killing off some vital aspects of one's 'self'*. Both Ogden and his patient had experienced, in this session, something very precious, that had been transformative to both. The reader, as many analysts, may be tempted to 'dissect' this conversation, interpret it, or try to 'understand' what went on in this session. The alternative is to read it and let it sink in, as quietly as possible, and observe the emotions that arise within us.

Chapter 3

Reading, Writing, and Practising Psychoanalysis

Ogden's identity is rooted in reading, writing, and practicing psychoanalysis. For him, these three pursuits have much in common. He has published more than eighty papers, some of which have been compiled into over fourteen books. In addition to his psychoanalytic writings, he has also written and published three books of prose. To him, writing and psychoanalysis are 'methods' of experiencing what is vital for *being alive*. It requires listening to the subtle echoes of sounds that have been 'lost'. The two papers I will discuss are "Listening—Three Frost poems" (1997a), and "A question of voice in poetry and psychoanalysis" (1998).

Ogden (1997a, p. 619) begins his paper with the following quote:

> You could ask what walks are good for ... Walks are useless. So are poems ... A walk doesn't mean anything, which is a way of saying that to some extent it means anything you can make it mean—and always more than you can make it mean ... Only uselessness is empty enough for the presence of so many uses ... Only uselessness can allow the walk to be totally itself.
>
> (A poem by A. R. Ammons, 1968)

The *experience* and one's ability for *experiencing* has a meaning in its own right, and it is almost always a meaning that is different, and *wider* than what we have imagined before. Ogden *experiences* language; he does not merely hear, or *understand'* it—language is an *object* that you should *sense*: "Of particular interest to me are

DOI: 10.4324/9781003388708-4

the *effects created by the sound* and meanings of these words and sentences and *the way language is used to create these effects"* (Ogden, 1997a, p. 620, italics added).

There is a relationship between the writer, the reader, and the language, with each of these creating (and re-creating) the other. Unless a text causes the reader to *feel something, meaning to experiencing an experience*, it is useless. Ogden discusses the *movement* or the *shift* that may occur in one's *experience* of something, and perhaps also the transformation that may occur as we get older. The young Ogden was "not taken" by his reading of Frost:

> The speaking voice seemed to present a narrative so clear that it seemed to leave me little to do as a reader. I was more drawn to "difficult" modern poets ... Frost is not a "difficult" poet in Eliot's sense of the word; his poetry does not dislocate by means of disjointed or absent narratives, fragmented images, obscure literary allusions and so on ... They are difficult in large part because they suggest formulae that won't formulate –that almost but don't quite formulate. I should like to be so subtle ... as to seem to the casual reader altogether obvious.
>
> (Frost, 1917, p. 692/Ogden, 1997a, pp. 621–22)

Ogden (2016a) discusses Winnicott's theory concerning the use of the object. Winnicott (2007) admits that:

> It appals me to think how much deep change I have prevented or delayed in patients in a certain classification category by my personal need to interpret. If only we can wait, the patient arrives at understanding creatively and with immense joy, *and I now enjoy this joy more than I used to enjoy the sense of having been clever.* I think I interpret mainly to let the patient know the limits of my understanding. The principle is that it is the patient and only the patient who has the answers.
>
> (Winnicott, 2007, pp. 86–87/Ogden, 2016a, p. 1244, italics added).

Ogden, too, has realized that a 'difficult' (i.e., 'clever') poet, or poetry, is not necessarily the most *effective* (and *affective)* one.

'Difficult' poetry demands a struggle to *understand,* whereas poetry that is *effective* allows the reader an *affective experience.* This is what Winnicott has realized, in the course of his career, in regard to the poetry of psychoanalysis: Winnicott's baby must destroy the mother as an *object,* re-creating her as a *subject,* paradoxically meaning that the baby is able to *accept* (and relate) to her as to an *external object,* that is *an object that it cannot control.* The relationship between the writer, the text, and the reader are the same—the writer and the reader have to accept one another as *external objects,* that is as *subjects,* in the sense that the writer cannot control how the text will be perceived, understood, or experienced by the reader, as much as the reader has to accept the limitations of his or her ability to be at one with the writer's intentions. Acknowledging and accepting the limitations of *understanding* and its' significance allows for new *forms of experiencing.*

On p. 622, Ogden discusses Forst's poem 'The Most of it', in which: "A man calls across a lake and bemoans the fact that nature merely offers up a 'mocking echo' and refuses to respond with a 'counter love' of its own".

The poem ends with the words "and that was all", reflecting, perhaps, on the humane encounter with the limits of one's own power and control over the external. But, if we agree to pause on these final words, we may be able to *experience* a wider range of emotions—the realization that a certain moment, or an experience, is *all* that there is to it may not only evoke disappointment, sadness or frustration, but also a sense of liberation and one's ability to truly appreciate what *is,* and not only what is *not.*

> The reader, like the man in the poem, cannot resist wishing the poem would "speak to him" and consequently attempts to make the words "and that was all" a memorable, simple truth that he can wrap up and take home with him. But the buck in the poem is more than a buck and less; it is *a buck that is the creation of the poem.* It is a buck that pushes "the crumpled water up ahead" and lands "pouring like a waterfall". It is not a buck "out there" *in nature,* but a buck created in the poem, through the sounds of *"newly made"* words and in *imaginative metaphors.*
>
> (pp. 622–623, italics added)

This is a complex and condensed passage, containing many of Ogden's theoretical and clinical thoughts. There is a parallel to be made between infant–mother, patient–analyst, and reader–writer. To grow up (psychologically and mentally), infant, patient, and reader must achieve emancipation, which often entails parental parricide (Loewald, 1979, Ogden, 2006). Infants, patients, and readers all attack their 'objects', once they experience the realization of "That is all?". It is this disappointment, and the emotions that follow it, which lead to the attempted destruction of the object. Ogden (2016a) suggests that this 'attempted destruction' is "the process of moving from object-relating to object-usage" (p. 1252). The infant's ability to use his maternal object, the patient's ability to use the analyst as an object and the reader's ability to use a poem as an 'object', utilized for the benefit of their psychological emotional growth is an achievement not to be taken for granted. It serves the patient's struggle to develop a *voice* of his/her own.

Ogden (1997a) chose three of Frost's poems because he "is fond of them" (p. 623), meaning:

Each has its own moments of *aliveness* and moments of flatness; *the parts that are most alive to me change over time.* It is important that the reader reads these poems aloud several times before going on to my discussion, for the poems *live in the sounds of the words and in what the words feel like in our mouth as we say them.*

(p. 624, italics added)

Understanding should follow one's *experience* and *experiencing;* first, the reader must *sense* the text (hearing and tasting the sounds). And it is precisely because this not 'possible' that it opens new possibilities for *creating something anew.* This is what poetry, writing, reading, and psychoanalysis is about—*experiencing something anew*, in a way that creates new (internal and external) possibilities. Ogden's *discussion* is like the analyst's *interpretations* or the patient's *understanding*—it is important, but it should only follow one's *experience.*

Ogden's analysis of the Frost's three poems concludes with what seems to me most important:

> Each of these poems (or rather the reader's experience of each poem) *is* the living event that the poem addresses, whether that be a particular experience of the love making and listening to poetry, or the struggle for and against words to bear witness to unspeakable experience, or the effort to keep alive in oneself what is most sacred over the course of a life. In each instance, the poem is not about an experience; the life of the poem is the experience.
>
> (p. 638, italics in original)

If one would not know that Ogden is writing about Frost and poetry, one could be certain he is writing about psychoanalysis. Analysts should not merely talk with their patients about what is going on—they must be able to be engaged participants in whatever it is that goes on. Psychoanalysis is, first and foremost, an *experience* and its most important goal is to facilitate the patient's capacity for *experiencing*. The *vital essence* of psychoanalysis is all that allows the patient to *be, and feel, alive*. Being alive requires *growing up*, meaning one must experience the (painful) disillusionment of omnipotence, meaning the acceptance (and mourning) of the limitations of our humane existence.

Ogden goes on to discuss the idea that he has discussed in the previous paper (1997a). In his paper "A question of voice in poetry and psychoanalysis" (1998) he points out the similarities and differences between the two. Ogden refers to two units, i.e., 'writer–reader' and 'analyst–patient', and to the way each of them is *using language as a way of creating the sense, and experience, of being alive*. Contemporary psychoanalytic methods, suggests Ogden, "over the last two decades have been moving in the direction of attending as closely to *the way* the analysand is *speaking* to *what* the analysand is *saying*" (p. 426, italics added).

The reader should take note of two shifts: (1) from 'what' to 'how', and (2) from 'speaking' to 'saying'. These shifts are from content to form and from interaction to attribution of meaning. Ogden focuses on one's *voice* and its double meaning; one's *voice* refers not only to *how* one *sounds* but also to one's *identity,* that is—who that person *is*: "Creating a voice with which to speak or to write might be thought of as a way, perhaps the principal way, in which *individuals bring themselves into being, come to life, through their use of language"* (pp. 426–427).

Ogden is putting forward four fundamentals of psychoanalysis and *being alive*: (1) it requires that a person has a voice of his/her own, i.e., *subjectivity*; (2) subjectivity is inseparable from coming into *being alive*; (3) creating a personal voice, i.e., *subjectivity*, has to do with being an *individual* (meaning it requires differentiation); and (4) it demands that one is able to *use language (*not merely *talk* or *speak*), that is *create meaning.*

The idea of having a (personal) *voice* is not the same as Winnicott's theory of true, or false self: "In an odd way, voice has qualities of both and at the same time and, in addition, might be viewed as a *medium for conscious and unconscious "experimentation" with the experience of the self"* (p. 427, italics added).

If Winnicott's 'true self' refers to where one is most *alive,* so do one's *speaking* and *writing*, offering the ability to carefully listen to one's own voice, which is at the same time *internal* and *external*:

> In the end, I believe that it is the *aliveness* of the voice created in *one's usage of language*, that is its own measure of *what feels most real.* Attending to the *aliveness* and *deadness* in the language *as experienced by writer/speaker and reader/listener* seems to me to be a more fruitful way of approaching the question of voice than through the more static motions of sincerity and insincerity, truth and deception.
>
> (p. 428)

Ogden offers here his shift from *true–false* to *aliveness–deadness.* This seems to be a shift not only away from epistemological psychoanalysis, but also an elaboration of Winnicott's thinking—the 'true self' is about one's feeling of *aliveness*, not about qualities that are 'truer' (or more sincere) than others. Ogden is putting forward the issue of aliveness *as the 'bedrock' of the psychoanalytic process.* The way one *uses language* is inseparable from *coming into life.* There is a continuous interdependence between

the voice of the writer and that of the reader, and this is also true
to the psychoanalytic setting:

> In an analytic setting, analyst and analysand together generate
> conditions in which each speaks with a *voice arising from the
> unconscious conjunction of the two individuals.* The voice of the
> analyst and the voice of the analysand under these circum-
> stances *are not the same voice,* but the two voices are spoken,
> to a significant degree, *from a common area of jointly (but
> asymmetrically) constructed unconscious experience.*
>
> (p. 444, italics added)

This is another implementation of Ogden's 'analytic third': each
analytic pair, and every unit of psychoanalysis develops a *voice of
its own.* This voice (that consists, for example, of specific habits,
opening and closing sentences, and other small things that feature
in that specific pair and analytic unit) is made up of the analyst's
voice and that of the patient; it is specific and particular to a specific analytic pair, unlike any other relationship the analyst may
have with his/her other patients, although some features will of
course be alike. Developing an individual *voice* is an *achievement*
(and this is also true when an analytic pair is concerned):

> Uniqueness of voice might be thought of as an *individual
> shape created in the medium of the use of the language.* This
> "shape" is one that is made not simply in the medium of
> language, *but in the medium of the use of language: voice is an
> action, not a potential, more verb than noun.*
>
> (p. 445, italics added)

There is an interesting idea in this elaboration of Ogden's idea of
'the use of the language-as-object', which is defined here not as
the end of the process, but as a *medium serving the individual in
achieving something else, i.e., greater aliveness.* The ultimate goal
(or hope) is that the baby (patient) will be able to *shape his/her
own voice* in a distinct way that makes each one of us *who we are.*
This refers also to the analyst's ability to achieve an independent,
and personal, perception of *what psychoanalysis is about,* and to

develop a personal analytic *style,* based on one's own experiences (as an analysand, supervisee, and analyst).

Clinical Illustrations—Finding the 'Voice' with and within Each Patient

Ogden (2016c) describes his analytic work with Mr. C, a patient with cerebral palsy. Ogden admits to having omnipotent wishes to 'cure' the patient of his illness, realizing with time that this served as a protection against the truth, that there was no way that he could 'cure' this patient of his physiological illness. Ogden describes some of the traumatic aspects of Mr. C's relationships with his mother, who couldn't accept him and his handicap: she raged at him and often insulted him, calling him a 'monster'. Ogden, of course, did not rage at or humiliate the patient in any way of form, but holding on to his 'omnipotent cure wishes' was *a form of not accepting the patient for who he really was.* It took Ogden a while, not only to accept the patient for who he really was, but also to be able to *love* him. In a later phase of his analysis, Mr. C told Ogden a dream he had the night before: ""Not much happened in the dream. I was myself with my cerebral palsy washing my car and enjoying listening to music on the car radio that I had turned up loud" (p. 25).

Not only was this the first time that the patient had referred to his cerebral palsy, while telling his analyst his dream, but Ogden refers to the specific *way* he was referring to it as "my cerebral palsy", representing the "depth of recognition and acceptance of himself" (p. 25). Ogden had experienced and understood the dream as the patient being able to

> *Be* a mother who took pleasure in bathing her baby (his car) while listening to and enjoying *the music that was coming from inside the baby.* This was not a dream of triumph; it was an ordinary dream of ordinary love: 'nothing much happened'.
>
> (p. 25, italics added)

Ogden, feeling very moved, responded by saying: "What a wonderful dream that was" (p. 25). Throughout his analysis, the patient was in a process of *finding his own voice*. Finding our own voice is essential to us *becoming a subject*. This is often a difficult and a painful process, as in the case of Mr. C, whose mother's voice was so unaccepting and insulting. In this dream, the patient not only finds a new voice—it is also his own ("my cerebral palsy"), and it is a loving voice, who can enjoy *being who he really is*. Ogden could have interpreted the dream, referring to various aspects of it, but he remained *true* to what the dream was about— a wordless (music) expression of simple love. Working with Mr. C had deepened Ogden's realization of the significance that truth has for our psychological growth:

> The idea that human beings have a powerful need for truth has further implications for me. The need for the truth is not a poli-cing function (keeping oneself honest); it is more an expression of a need for the *"freedom to think"* the reality of one's experi-ence (Symington, 1983), which is essential to psychoanalysis as a therapeutic process. My role as an analyst is to help the patient mature in ways that allow him to better encompass the realities of his emotional life. *Helping a patient face the truth of his experience need not be a confrontational experience. I do not point out the truth to the patient, I live it with the patient* until he or she is able to experience it on his own and express it in verbal or nonverbal ways. Integral to facing the truth is the patient's trust in me, and my trustworthiness.
>
> (Ogden, 2016b, p. 26, italics added)

Ogden's *truth* is rooted in his ability to *experience* the patient's truth, or the truth of what is happening in the session, meaning that he is able (and willing) to *live an experience with the patient*. This is not only a specific *way* of *conducting an analysis*, but also a *way of using language,* "not just a basket in which ideas are carried; the way in which language is used to state an idea is inseparable from the content of the idea" (p. 26). In what comes next, Ogden is making another step in defining ontological psychoanalysis:

> The acts of *"explaining"* and *"understanding"* have always felt like very different categories of experience, but recently the

differences between the two have served to highlight principles of practice that are particularly important to me. A stereotypic example of explaining something to a patient might sound like this: "I think that you overslept this morning and missed most of the session because your expression of gratitude to me as you left our session yesterday frightened you." A principal shortcoming, to my mind, in this interpretation, even if it were in some sense accurate, is that it objectifies the patient. The analyst is talking *about* the patient, not with the patient. The explanation relies heavily on conscious, secondary process thinking even as it purports to address the workings of the patient's unconscious. Human response to experience does not obey the laws of *cause and effect* logic or of sequential time. *We are the totality of our life's experience as we live the present moment. The past is not "behind us", it is in us. The unconscious is not "timeless", it is full of time (the entirety of our lives).*

(p. 28, italics added)

Unlike *explaining* and *understanding,* Ogden (following Winnicott) is suggesting that understanding should only follow the analyst's and patient's experience of *living an experience together.* Understanding, and the experience of *being understood* is an intimate experience, which is paradoxical; as intimate as it is, it consists of the patient's and analyst's experience (e.g., acknowledgement and acceptance) of being two separate people. This kind of *understanding* and *feeling, or being understood is:*

An ontological phenomenon, an experience in which an aspect of one's essential being is recognized by another person. This can be achieved only in a relationship in which there is, for both patient and analyst, a feeling of profound trust.

(p. 29)

Clinical Illustration

Mr. V (Ogden 2016b, p. 31) was in analysis for a year, when, upon meeting him in the waiting room, Ogden recalled a dream he had the previous night. Ogden had dreamt that he was with a group of people who were fleeing, not completely *knowing* why, but with a clear feeling that they had done something terribly wrong, perhaps even committed a murder. The police were coming after them, with the intention of killing or imprisoning them. Ogden then found himself, alone, facing a policeman, at whom he was pointing a gun. Ogden was struck by the realization that the policeman not only seemed to be a small boy, but was also completely unarmed. Pointing the gun at the policeman, Ogden was trying to make up his mind whether to shoot him or not. He then woke up with his heart pounding.

When meeting Mr. V in the waiting room the next morning, Ogden recalled the dream but could not 'understand' why. In the session, Mr. V, who had seldom talked about his brother, mentioned his name for the first time. He told Ogden that his brother Paul had called him the evening before: "It's always upsetting to talk to him. It isn't actually having a conversation with anyone. He talks a mile a minute and I just listen. I can't understand most of what he's talking about" (p. 31).

The patient then told Ogden that his brother Paul was considered, as a young boy, to be very clever and artistic, but had suffered a schizophrenic breakdown during his first year at college. Following his breakdown, he was never able to hold on to a job for more than a short while, had never married, and lived off welfare and the support their parents. Ogden then recalled the young policeman from his dream—a boy he had to decide whether to kill, fearing the policeman would otherwise kill him or imprison him. At that point, Ogden seemed to have been drifting away in thoughts about the analysis: He felt upset, recounting some of his past interventions with this patient. Specifically, he felt disappointed with some of his interpretations, feeling that they were merely a *disguise for not knowing* what else to do. Ogden had realized that those interpretations were, in fact, a disguise for *feeling lost*. He went on to think about the specific way in which the patient was handling his own feelings of being lost, often referring to Ogden as if he had no *knowledge* or *understanding* of literature, art, or music. Ogden and the patient were silent for a while, and then Mr. V said:

I don't know why I feel responsible for Paul. I was at a different college from the one where he fell apart. I only found out about it after he was hospitalized. They moved him to a mental hospital in the middle of nowhere. So, I couldn't visit him. *That's not true*, I could have visited, but I didn't want to see him in a mental hospital.

(p. 31, italics added)

Ogden's dream, from the night before, and the new 'truths' that came out in this session are interconnected. Not only did the patient refer to his brother by name for the first time, but he was also able to talk about feeling responsible and 'betraying' his brother by not visiting him in hospital. Ogden's dream was also the patient's (undreamt) dream—conveying the deep truth of being so intimidated by his brother's illness, feeling it is a struggle of life and death. Ogden's dream, and what happened in the next day session, allowed for new 'truths' to come out and be experienced, not only by the patient, but also by Ogden, who was able to feel more compassion towards Mr. V's condescension, viewing it, from then on, as the patient's efforts to shore up his self-esteem. Ogden had a feeling that Mr. V had been afraid to tell him (and perhaps himself as well) that he himself has suffered a breakdown as a child, from which he had never healed. Ogden 'imagined' (dreamt) that the patient's breakdown went unnoticed by his parents, and he was left to 'carry it' by himself, all alone:

"They" did not know what was happening with him (and perhaps did not want to know)—just as he saw me as knowing nothing about literature, music, and so on, and *just as the boy and I, in "my dream," were absolutely alone in the face of matters of life-and-death importance* (to "lose one's mind" is to lose oneself, which is equivalent to losing one's life).

(p. 32, italics added)

The analyst's dream and reverie facilitate an emotional experience, leading to some new *understandings*. These *understandings* are not necessarily 'factual reality', but are nonetheless important. They are psychic-emotional *truths* that enable us to better hold and contain our experiences. Mr. V held difficult truths, concerning his own breakdown, his brother's illness, his inability to be in touch with it, and his feeling that he needed to protect himself; he wanted (and perhaps *needed*) to face the truth and, at the same time, was utterly anxious to do so. Facing the truth is not easy, and Mr. V, as do many of us, needed his analyst to *live this truth (experience) with him*. Psychoanalysis, in many ways is a place of "working at the frontier of yet-to-be-known truths of human experience, a place that is constantly engendering wonder and humility" (p. 34).

Analysts and patients develop a unique, and a personal *way of talking with one another*. In his paper "How I talk *with* my patients" (2018c, italics added), Ogden provides an important discussion of this evolution of analytic style:

> Perhaps the most important clinical questions, and the most difficult ones for me as a practicing psychoanalyst, are those not so much concerned with *what* I say to my patients, as they are with *how* I talk with my patients. In other words, my focus over the years has moved from *what I mean* to *how I mean*. Of course, the two are inseparable, but in this paper, I place emphasis on the latter.
>
> (p. 399, italics in original)

This is a relatively early declaration of Ogden's ontological perspective, putting the emphasis on the *experience* (e.g. the *how*), rather than on *knowing* or *understanding*. Psychoanalysis cannot be *generalized* but must be *reinvented* anew with each patient. Analysts necessarily make mistakes and *do not understand* their patients or what, exactly, is happening in the session. These 'mistakes' are what opens up possibilities for new experiences and understandings, for both patient and analyst. It is impossible to always, and immediately, be able to communicate an experience—hence, both patient and analyst need to be able *to live it, first, together*.

What analysts and patients *can* do is "to communicate *something like* our lived experiences by re-presenting the experience" (p. 400, italics in original). This may be expressed by using a particular phrase, metaphor, irony, etc. Within each session there are two subjectivities, and this is not a 'problem' that needs 'to be solved,' but rather—"it is a space in which a dialectic of separateness and intimacy may give rise to creative expression" (p. 400). However, there are always parts and pieces that are left out of the patient–analyst communication:

> Paradoxically, the parts that are missing, the parts left out of our communications open a space in which we may be able, in some way, to bridge the gap between ourselves and others. The patient's experience of *being creative* in the act of communicating is an essential part of the process of his "dreaming himself more fully into existence" (Ogden 2004b, p. 858), coming into being in a way that is uniquely his own.
>
> (Ogden, 2018c, p. 401, italics in original)

The parts that are left out of the patient–analyst communication are, most often, the most important parts of this communication—being what the patient and/or analyst are not yet aware of, or do not *know* yet. It is this 'void' that can create an open space for *dreaming new dreams* and for the *experiencing* of *new experiences*.

Asking the patient some 'direct' questions (e.g., "Why have you been so quiet today?" or "Why have you skipped the previous session?") usually lead to 'conscious' answers, detailing some concrete reasoning or other information which is more 'on the surface' of the patient's awareness, meaning *cause-and-effect*, secondary processes of *explanation*. This, suggests Ogden, is usually connected to an *unconscious aspect* (of what it is that is occurring at that moment), which is *frightening* for the analyst (or patient). Asking specific questions, or responding in specific ways, is usually connected to a *specific, theoretical technique* that is connected to a specific analytic *school*. Ogden prefers an analytic style that is based on: "one's own personal creation that is loosely based on existing principles of analytic practice, but more importantly is a living process that has its origins in the personality and experience of the analyst" (p. 402).

This takes us back to Ogden's paper (2006) of Loewald's reconstructed oedipal theory of how each generation's need to re-invent anew consists of the 'killing' of the previous generation. Yet, this 'killing' is not perceived as a murderous act, but as an act of creating-anew, meaning it is not about the killing of something old, but about the need of creating something new, meaning it is an act of *living* and of *being alive.* This is present not only in the way each analyst becomes himself or herself in the process of growing up, being different than one's own analyst, but it also comes into being in the way we are *different* with each of our patients, creating ourselves anew in each session.

Many of our patients have experienced a profound loneliness during their childhood, having had the experience that they cannot *really* talk with their parents, often leading to feelings of being trapped. Such painful and frightening feelings are inevitable within the patient–analyst relationship, that is within the transfer-ence–countertransference. Yet:

> The patient may also be able to sense that in some way he is *no longer as utterly alone as he once was.* Secondly, the patient *is no longer a child* and is in possession of psychic capacities for handling the threat to his sanity and his life that he did not have available to him as a child. These felt differences have provided an important underpinning of hope in the analyses I have conducted.
>
> (Ogden, 2018c, p. 403, italics added)

Here lies another profound paradox of psychoanalysis. On the one hand, some key aspects of the patient's past traumas must be re-experienced within the analytic relationship, but on the other hand, there need to be some *vital* differences, so the patient can experience the (present) trauma in a way that would allow psychological growth. This is often made possible because the patient is not *as alone* as she or he was in infancy or childhood, and because in the years that have passed, since the patient was a baby, she or he *has acquired* some new ways of *being.* The analytic situation must be similar enough, yet different enough, to create a *space* in which old and new experiences can be experiences as *new.*

An important shift, emphasised by Ogden, is the shift from *explaining* to *describing*. Describing, unlike explaining, frees both patient and analyst to *not understand:*

> An example of describing instead of explaining took place in an initial analytic meeting. Earlier in my development as an analyst, if a patient in an initial meeting were to begin by telling me that she felt terrified by coming to see me, I might have asked, "*What terrifies you?*" or "*Why are you terrified?*" More recently, when a patient began by telling me she was terrified to come to see me, I said, "*Of course you are*".
>
> (p. 404, italics added)

Ogden's response "Of course you are" can be thought of a "description-in-action" (p. 404), meaning that Ogden is accepting the patient for who she is, that she is terrified of him. By accepting this for what it is, the analyst allows the patient to *feel* that no explanations are needed at that moment, and that *experiencing* her feelings are as important as *understanding* them. The analyst needs not to reassure the patient by *constantly explaining* to the patient what she or he is feeling.

Describing Rather than Explaining—A Clinical Illustration

On pp. 404–405 Ogden describes an example of a descriptive intervention: Mr. M was in analysis for a few years when, in his session, he told Ogden of a dream he was telling his wife about, in which their son had died. His wife immediate reaction was: "Stop. I don't want to hear any more", to which Ogden reacted by saying "good for her" (p. 405). This was a spontaneous reaction, that may seem odd to some analysts. Yet Ogden had the feeling that just as all the figures in a patient's dream are aspects of the patient's self, so are all the figures that come up in the story (or associations) that follow the dream, meaning that the wife's declaration that she does not want to hear anything else about the patient's dream is representing as aspect of the patient's self. The patient's reaction to Ogden's intervention proved that Ogden's feeling (or intuition) was true—the patient said he felt relieved when his wife interrupted his account of his dream. This was also perceived as a sign of the patient's analytic progress—being able to interrupt his own obsessive unwanted thoughts and evacuation of them onto others.

Ogden seems to 'understand' that:

> We all speak with a simultaneous wish to be understood and to be misunderstood, and that we listen to others both with the desire to understand and to misunderstand. The latter—the wish to misunderstand and be misunderstood—only in part reflects a desire not to be known, a desire to maintain an aspect of self that stands in necessary isolation (as described by Winnicott 1963).
>
> (Ogden, 2018c, p. 412)

Being 'not understood' allows us to keep our private self to ourselves and draws an important distinction between 'me' and 'not me'. It allows the patient the *independence* she or he needs to become her or his own self:

> The wish to be understood inherently carries a wish for closure, a wish to be recognized for who one is at present. By contrast, I find that the patient's wish to be misunderstood involves a wish to dream herself up (as opposed to being seen by the analyst). Respecting the patient's need for self-discovery places a demand on me not to "know too much".
>
> (p. 412)

It may be that both states of (1) feeling not understood, when one wishes to be understood, and (2) being understood, when one wishes to be not understood, are states in which the patient feels impinged upon by the analyst. Being misunderstood by the analyst allows the patient to discover and express some nuance of her or his experience, allowing for new communication. Analysis is a never-ending discourse between *understanding* and *not understanding,* on behalf of the analyst, and the patient's *experience* of *feeling or being understood* and *feeling or being misunderstood.* Although *understanding* may often limit and inhabit the analyst's and patient's scope of possible *experiencing*, we should think of these experiences (e.g. both understanding and not understanding) as vitally important for the patient's psychological growth, enabling diverse *experiences* of *intimacy* (understanding) and *differentiation*, (not understanding), of *dreaming together* and *separately*.

Chapter 4

Ontological Psychoanalysis— The Re-Creation and Experiencing of Something (A)New

In 2019, Ogden published what he considers to be one of his most important papers: "Ontological psychoanalysis or 'What do you want to be when you grow up?'" In this paper, Ogden distinguishes between two types of psychoanalysis: (1) epistemological psychoanalysis—whose main contributors are Freud and Klein; and (2) ontological psychoanalysis—whose main contributors are Winnicott and Bion.

For Ogden, ontological psychoanalysis represents a significant shift in the focus of psychoanalytic theory and technique. *Epistemological psychoanalysis,* focused on *knowing* and *understanding,* is primarily concerned with *uncovering hidden meanings, interpreting unconscious conflicts, and understanding how past experiences shape current perceptions and behaviours.* Ogden considers Freud and Klein to be the founders of epistemological psychoanalysis and Winnicott and Bion the founders of *ontological psychoanalysis,* which, in contrast, concentrates on the patients' *experience of being, sense of self, and how they come into existence as a person.* Ontological psychoanalysis addresses questions of *authenticity, aliveness,* and the process of *becoming.* Although it is important to remember that epistemological and ontological psychoanalysis do not exist in pure form, distinguishing between the two schools is important: "Epistemological psychoanalysis, as I am using the term, refers to a process of gaining knowledge and arriving at *understandings* of the patient, particularly understandings of the patient's unconscious inner world and its relation to the external world. (p. 663, italics added).

DOI: 10.4324/9781003388708-5

At the heart of epistemological psychoanalysis is *interpretation,* specifically interpretation of the *transference:* "The analyst conveys in words to the patient his or her understanding of the ways in which the patient is experiencing the analyst as if he or she were a real or imagined figure from the patient's infancy or childhood. (p. 664).

Within the transference–countertransference, patients are experiencing, in the present, past experiences that they 'need' to re-experience. Yet, the patient's experiencing is perceived as a means to the end of *understanding.*

In contrast to epistemological psychoanalysis, when Ogden talks about ontological psychoanalysis, he is referring: "to a dimension of psychoanalysis in which the analyst's primary focus is on facilitating the patient's efforts to become more fully himself" (p. 664).

This position is a reference to Winnicott's distinction (1971a) between the *symbolic meaning* of *play* and the patient's *state* of being that has to do with *playing.* Epistemological psychoanalysis is about *symbolic meaning* and *play,* whereas ontological psychoanalysis focuses on the patient's (and analyst's) *being* and *playing.* Ogden cites Winnicott (1971a), suggesting that, from an ontological perspective:

Psychotherapy takes place in the overlap of two areas of play-ing, that of the patient and that of the therapist. The corollary to this is that where playing is not possible then the work done by the therapist is directed towards bringing the patient from a state of not being able to play into a state of being able to play.
(Winnicott 1971a, p. 38, italics in the original,/Ogden 2019, p. 664)

Ogden is connecting *playing* with *dreaming*, and the 'analytic third' with the ontological emphasis on *experience* and *experiencing*. An epistemological analyst focuses on conveying his *understanding* through the means of *interpretation*, and the ontological psycho-analyst waits before conveying his *understanding* to the patient. It is the experience of the patient which is more important than the analyst's conveying of his *knowledge* and *understanding*: "'Arriv[ing] at understanding creatively and with immense joy', an experience in which the patient is engaged not predominantly in searching for self-understanding, but in experiencing the process of becoming more fully himself" (p. 665).

The analyst, being a good enough environmental mother, 'co-creates' the conditions that the patient needs for *arriving* at her or his own *understanding*. Winnicott and Ogden are both talking about an *on-going* process that consists of *playing, together* and *separately*. Winnicott's emphasis is on *dreaming* and he distinguishes it from *fantasying:*

> For me the work of this session had produced an important result. It had taught me that *fantasying* interferes with *action* and with *life in the real or external world*, but much more so ... it interferes with *dream[ing]* and with the *personal or inner psychic reality*, the living core of the individual personality.
> (Winnicott, 1971a, p. 31/Ogden, 2019, p. 665, italics added)

Rarely do psychoanalysts prefer "action" or "life in the real or external world" to "fantasying". Winnicott's original thinking is profoundly evident here: "fantasying" is not the same as fantasy, and he considers it not only a waste of time, but a real interference, hindering one's aliveness, having little to do with one's "personal or inner psychic reality", which is the "living core of the individual personality". Ogden emphasizes the significance of our ability to weave objects that are 'not-me' into our internal world, e.g., our personality or our personal patterns. We can think about this ability as the ability for playing or dreaming, which is vital for our psychological growth:

> When the patient or analyst is *unable to engage in playing*, the analyst's attention must be directed to this *problem*, for it *precludes the patient and analyst from experiencing "the overlap of two areas of playing"*. If the analyst is unable to engage in playing, he must determine whether his inability to engage in this state of being (playing is not simply a state of mind, it is a state of being) is a reflection of what is occurring between him and the patient (possibly a profound identification with the patient's lifelessness) or a reflection of his own inability to genuinely engage in playing, which would likely require that he return to analysis.
> (p. 666, italics added)

Playing is one of the most significant achievements we can hope for, in terms of one's ability to be *alive* and to *experiencing one's aliveness*. Winnicott places playing in the "overlap of two areas", which is where Ogden places 'dreaming', 'reverie' and the 'analytic third'. Playing and dreaming are not *activities*, but *states of being, experiencing and creating something that often contains tension of opposites, such as it is both, and at the same time, it is personal and separated, as much as it is mutual and together*. It holds (and contains), both and at the same time, aspects of the patient's (and analyst's) past and present, meaning that it is both a 'recreation' and something that is newly created. These (as-if) contradictions are not to be decided on; what is important is the ability to *hold* and *contain* the *dialectic tension*. Ogden is aware of the vast overlap between the two schools, that of epistemological and that of ontological psychoanalysis, meaning a verbal interpretation may lead to a significant *experience* on behalf of the patient, just as much as *experiencing* may lead to a greater *understanding* of both patient and analyst. Yet: "There are a great many experiences that occur in the course of an analysis that are predominantly epistemological or predominantly ontological in nature. (p. 667).

Ogden argues that epistemological and ontological psychoanalysis differ in their therapeutic techniques—and I would add in their means and perhaps even goals. Epistemological psychoanalysis is focused on the attempted *understanding* specifically of unconscious thoughts, feelings, or somatic experiences, while the aim of ontological psychoanalysis is the provision of interpersonal context to facilitate *experience* and the patient's *experiencing*.

For Ogden, psychoanalysis (and specifically ontological psychoanalysis) is about *being* and *feeling alive*. He bases his theory of ontological psychoanalysis on Winnicott's and Bion's thinking. Winnicott's paper (1971b) "Transitional objects and transitional phenomena" is especially significant to Ogden's ontological perspective, in which Winnicott describes:

… an intermediate state of experiencing, to which inner reality and external life both contribute. It is an area that is not challenged, because no claim is made on its behalf except that it shall exist as a resting-place for the individual engaged in the perpetual human task of keeping inner and outer reality separate yet interrelated.

(Winnicott, 1971b, p. 2/(Ogden, 2019, p. 668)

The infant's capacity to *experience* a *state of being*, requires that it is capable of *experiencing transitional phenomena and/or objects,* and this demands that the mother is capable of such a *state of being*, not asking the baby whether the object was *found* or *created*. This is a paradoxical state, in which the mother *knows* that the object was there to be found, yet allows the baby the illusion of *creating it anew*. Winnicott relates this state of being to "arts, religion and to imaginative living" (Winnicott 1971b, p. 14), and Ogden connects it to Winnicott's thinking on the core of the uncommunicative self:

> The non-communicating central self, for ever immune from the reality principle [immune to the need to respond to anything external to the self], and for ever silent. *Here communication is not non-verbal; it is, like the music of the spheres, absolutely personal.* It belongs to being alive. And in health, it is out of this that communication naturally arises.
>
> (Winnicott, 1963, p. 192/Ogden, 2019, p. 669, italics added)

The connection that Ogden makes between transitional phenomena, the non-communicating core of the self, and ontological psychoanalysis is significant; it allows and even promotes a psychoanalytic approach according to which he is not only suggesting that not each experience of the patient must be verbalized, but that it may even be necessary that some would remain unsaid. Putting any experience into words takes something away from that experience, as one can never express the nuances of the emotional or bodily experience exactly as it is. Often, the communication with another person is worth this abstraction, but not always. The silence that lies at the core of our self is not a not a verbal silence, but neither is it a 'non-verbal' silence; it is beyond verbal, and beyond human comprehension, and this is how it should *be*. Winnicott equates it to "the music of the spheres, absolutely personal". This is where we are *most alive* and should not be shared with anyone.

Other than Winnicott, Bion is the theorist that Ogden perceives as most valuable to the development of ontological thinking: "Just as Winnicott shifted the focus of analysis from play to playing, Bion shifted the analytic focus from (the understanding of) dreams to (the experience of) dreaming (which, for Bion, is synonymous with doing unconscious psychological work)" (p. 670).

Bion, suggests Ogden, insists that psychoanalysis should not be about *understanding,* but rather about one's *"experience of being"* (p. 670, italics in original). Going back to Bion's paper "Notes on memory and desire" (1967 [2013]), Ogden relates Bion's insistence that the analyst's focus should be on the *here and now* to focus on *experience* and *experiencing.* The analyst must be able and willing to renounce *knowing* and *understanding,* and replace them with *intuiting* what is happening in the session: "He *"intuits"* it, he *becomes "at one"* with it, he is *fully present in experiencing the present moment."* (p. 670, italics added)

This state of *experiencing* and *being* often requires that analyst can use his or her *reveries:* "Reverie (waking-dreaming) is a state of being that entails making oneself unconsciously receptive to experiencing what is so disturbing to the patient (or infant) that he is unable to "dream" (to do unconscious psychological work with) the experience" (p. 670).

Reveries are the mother–analyst's way of *experiencing* what the baby–patient is unable to contain (unbearable emotional and/or somatic experiences). The mother–analyst uses her or his mature capabilities to process what is indigestible to the baby–patient. Following this processing, the mother–analyst then transforms the digested experience for the baby–patient. Bion uses the terminology of *states of being* and *dreaming* to describe mental health and pathologies, for example he defines psychosis as a state of being in which the patient cannot fall asleep or wake up, meaning he or she cannot dream, i.e., no unconscious psychological work is possible.

Ogden is making an interesting connection between Winnicott's *going on being* and Bion's conceptualization of the baby's state of mind, prior to the transformation of beta-elements, meaning that in both states the baby does not have the ability for subjectivity of its own. In both states, it is the mother that is 'responsible' for sparing the baby the hard work of 'thinking,' or having to process what is yet too difficult. Winnicott's mother lends her baby her subjectivity, and Bion's mother lends her baby her alpha-function. If the baby receives the right amount of this maternal care and assistance, it will eventually be able to produce its *dream thoughts*, resulting in the baby's ability to become a *subject* in its own right. *Being a subject* allows us to *experience ourselves as alive and real*.

Ontological Psychoanalysis—Clinical Illustrations

In his paper (2019) Ogden gives a few very brief examples of *ontological interventions*. The first is of a thirty-year-old patient, whose relationship with his father was not good for a while, and they were not speaking to one another for a whole year. Towards the end of the session, Ogden said to the patient: "Haven't you had enough of this?" (p. 675). This intervention was not an interpretation, neither was it aimed at the patient's *understanding* of what was going on between him and his father. Rather, it was meant to convey Ogden's feeling that not talking to his father had become the patient's *state of being*, which no longer reflected who he was and who he had *become*. This intervention affected the patient deeply, altering "something fundamental to who the patient was' (p. 675).

Another example is that of Ms. L who, at her first session with Ogden, burst into tears, saying, "I am terrified by being here," to which Ogden had replied "Of course you are." Again, *choosing* to *not interpret* the patient's terror allows her experience to take centre stage. This simple acknowledgment and acceptance of the patient's *emotional state* allows a different discourse between patient and analyst.

In one of his recent papers, Ogden (2024b) questions the concepts of the *unconscious* and that of *analytic time*. Ogden dares to suggest that "there is no such entity as the unconscious" (p. 279). Regardless of how central this concept is in psychoanalytic thinking, it is "just an idea" (p. 279). For Ogden, even one's dreams are not proof of the existence of the unconscious: "The dreams one remembers are conscious phenomena and those one cannot remember are forgotten thoughts like other thoughts or experiences that one cannot remember" (p. 280).

Ogden is suggesting that the concept of the 'unconscious' is an *idea* that helps us to better "understand the meanings of our experience" (p. 280), specifically the experiences "that lie beyond conscious awareness" (p. 280). Ogden insists on clarifying that psychoanalytic concepts, regardless of how helpful they are to us, should be understood as *ideas*, or *metaphors*:

> There is no "inner world" (inside what?), nor are there object relationships inside of it, nor are there alpha-elements, beta-elements, alpha-function; there is no id, ego, or superego, no life instinct and death instinct, and so on. All of these are characters are forces and organizers in stories written by psychoanalysts.
>
> (p. 280)

It is important that we do not understand these concepts as absolute truths or concrete domains, they are *meanings* created by us, with the purpose of helping us to better comprehend something and to be able to share these understandings with others, but they are not evidence of anything. The concept of the 'unconscious' is central to our psychoanalytic thinking, but it is not a place or a domain. Rather, Ogden defines the unconscious as "*a quality of one's thinking, feeling, and experiencing*" (p. 281, italics added).

Ogden uses the term 'consciousness' to refer to "everything we are capable of experiencing, all of our thoughts, feelings, sensations, and, as development proceeds, the capacity for self-reflection in which there is an "I" as subject, and a "me" as object" (p. 281).

Ogden differentiates Freud's 'unconscious' from his own conceptualization of 'consciousness': at first, 'consciousness' refers to one's ability to experience thoughts, emotions or sensations. At a more developed stage, it refers to one's ability for self-reflection and to the ability to engage in self-talk, meaning that one is both an object and a subject.

The 'Unconscious' as an Idea—Clinical Illustration

Ogden presents the first encounter he had with Ms. V, in his waiting room. As he entered the waiting room, Ms. V stood up, abruptly, and looked up, directly into his eyes, pleadingly. Ogden describes Ms. V as a young woman, in her twenties, "dressed in a plain blouse and pleated skirt that were strikingly unfashionable" (p. 282). Following Ogden's introduction of himself, the patient followed him into his office, waiting for him to tell her where she should sit. She sat down and then told Ogden that she was told that she must leave her doctoral program. She then paused, as if waiting for further instructions.

Ogden's response to this was, saying to her: "It's natural not to know what you're supposed to do here" (p. 282). Ms. V then told Ogden that she was told to leave her studies for "failure to follow instructions" (p. 282). She then added that she had been working in a high-end fashion store and was encountering difficulties because she "always seems to be saying the wrong thing" (p. 282). Ms. V then further elaborated:

> I'm always saying the wrong thing. I end up insulting custo-
> mers when I'm only trying to help them find something they
> like. That's what happens but I don't want it to. My mother
> hates me. I'm not like her. I'm not feminine enough or pretty
> enough for her. I should be skinnier. She hates fat people. She
> likes my younger sister. My father loves me. He lets me go on
> rounds with him at the hospital. I'm too old for that, I know,
> but I did it as a kid and I've never wanted to give it up.
>
> (p. 283)

She then stopped and asked Ogden: "Aren't you supposed to ask me questions?", to which Ogden replied: "To tell you the truth, I don't know what I am supposed to do."

The patient then changed the subject and went on to tell Ogden how she used to do rounds with her physician father, at the hospital, playing the role of his nurse and how her mother was upset with her for doing so. Ogden acknowledged her experience of being someone *meaningful* when she was pretending to be a nurse assisting her father. Then, the patient, once again, changed the topic, asking Ogden whether he had read all the books in his office, to which Ogden replied: "Most of them." The patient then made an observation, saying to Ogden: "You are old." (p. 283), to which he responded by saying: "Yes, I am." The patient's next association referred to the 'fact' that her mother had never played with her.

The conversation between Ms. V and Ogden goes on, and what is most striking about it is that it does not include any interpretations; Ogden and Ms. V *talk with one another* in a way that resembles Winnicott's *squiggle game.* This game begins from the moment Ogden and Ms. V meet in Ogden's waiting room, when she looks, pleadingly, at him, waiting for him to give her instructions as to how she should behave. Ogden senses this and 'refuses' to give her instructions, facilitating an *experience of playing together.* Playing is the opposite of being instructed, it is about *being real.* The patient plays along, saying what is really on her mind, not being chained by the need to be polite. Telling Ogden that he is old is not meant as an insult; it is a simple observation and the fact that Ogden is able to 'play along', not adding any interpretations to what the patient is saying, allows a free-style movement, like a pendulum that is moving from Ms. V to Ogden, back and forth.

The choice *not to interpret* is a choice to not address, or focus, on the *unconscious latent meanings that lie beneath (or behind) what the patient is saying.* This does not mean that the analyst is oblivious to the possible hidden (repressed, unconscious) aspects of what the patient is saying. Rather, it may be that the analyst is responding to the 'hidden' aspects in the *way* she or he responds to the patient. In the example of Ms. V, it seems to me that Ogden *sensed* the patient's need to be *seen* and *accepted* for who *she really was.* The 'squiggle' communication that Ogden facilitated was a *de facto acceptance* of the patient's need to not follow instructions: Instead of interpreting the patient's way of *being seen,* Ogden *actualized* this in the session, *by the way he communicated* with her, creating a *mutual experience,* which the two of them were able *to live together:*

> In the session I have described, I was engaged with Ms V not primarily in an effort to *understand* her, but in *an effort to recognize her, to see her for who she was.* The need to be seen by another person is necessary to one's gaining a sense of who one is. One cannot become anyone without being seen,

beginning with the infant's experience of seeing him- or herself reflected in what the mother sees in the infant as she looks at him or her (Winnicott, 1967). *The need to be seen is not a conscious or an unconscious wish, it is an existential need.* In working with Ms V, I was engaged not primarily in enhancing her self-understanding, but in seeing her, recognizing her, and inviting her to play with me.

(p. 285, italics added)

Ontological psychoanalysis does not deny the significance of the *'unconscious'* as a concept that can help the analyst to think about what may be happening in the session, but it is not its focus. We may, naturally, think about the oedipal aspects of the patient's pretending to be a nurse assisting her father, or her difficulties to follow the rules as manifestations of her repressed (unconscious) anger, etc. Yet Ogden's main response to "Why not make use of the concept of the unconscious?" (p. 285) is that:

Doing so in a consistent way is to become locked in a state of mind in which one is engaged in a search for answers to questions concerning latent meaning. To be engaged in a search for unconscious meaning may eclipse a state of mind in which one is concerned not with answering questions about unconscious meaning, but concerned with the patient's difficulty in coming into being as him- or herself, difficulty in experiencing him- or herself as real, not knowing who one is, feeling that one is nobody, and so on.

(p. 285)

Ontological psychoanalysis is concerned with the *experience of becoming one's real self*, more than with the achievement of greater *understanding*, although, as I have said before, they *are* mutually interconnected.

In this paper (2024b), Ogden goes on to discuss the issue of 'analytic time' (p. 285). Ogden describes two different time-related experiences: that of 'diachronic time' (p. 285), which concerns 'clock time', meaning external (objective) time, and that of 'synchronic time', meaning 'dream time':

Diachronic time is sequential and closely associated with cause-and-effect logic. One experience follows another … Diachronic time is an experience in which there is separation of inside and outside, self and other. The internal and external are in a relationship of mutual influence, for example: the patient felt exposed by the analyst's ending the meeting in a way that felt abrupt, although she felt she may have been over-reacting.

(pp. 285–6)

Unlike 'diachronic time', which is the time of developmental sequence, 'synchronic time' might be thought of as 'dream time', (p. 286), meaning it may hold still and move rapidly at the same time, as it is gathered onto the *present moment*. This, says Ogden, is the *experience of time* while painting, playing, reading, writing, etc. Much of our work as psychoanalysts is to facilitate the conditions under which the patient can let go of 'diachronic time' in favour of *experiencing* 'synchronic time'. Although synchronic experience of time is inseparable from a diachronic experience, these experiences are different: Synchronic time lacks a past, 'accepting' that the past is gone and can only exist in the form of memories. Yet, the past is present and contained in the present moment by means of the impressions it has inscribed onto the individual; it is *alive* in one's feelings, bodily sensations and memories. Ogden conceives this as an important paradox—the past is merely a memory, yet it is *alive* in the present moment, *in the way the individual is.* This experience is evident in traumatic memories—although the traumatic event itself is over, its memory is being experienced as being completely *alive* in the 'here and now' of the session.

Ogden does not perceive patients as 'regressing' to a past phase, but rather as *living an experience (that has to do with their past), experiencing it as something that is happening now.* This *enlivened experience* is not an exact repetition of past event, but a *new creation, mutually facilitated by both patient and analyst.* The fact that the analyst is present with the patient makes a substantial difference to the patient's experience, and alters it. Ogden suggests that this perspective changes the way we may perceive transference; rather than being perceived as the patient's projection of past object-related experiences, from the perspective of 'synchronic time', the patient and the analyst are *living together an experience.* Following Winnicott's theory of mental breakdowns (1974), Ogden perceives the analytic relationship as a 'place' where past experiences, which the patient was unable to *experience,* are brought up so the patient can *live through them* with the analyst. It is in this sense, too, that these experiences are *new* to the patient.

Analytic Time—Clinical Illustration

Ms. C, an analysand of Ogden, experienced herself as a 'visitor' in her own life. She seemed to have no idea how she should behave as a wife or mother, and leaned on Ogden to help her through the day. Regardless of her profound dependency on others, including her analyst, she did not trust him, being extremely critical of him and everything he said or did. Although she, for example, arrived at each of her sessions fifteen minutes early, she once told Ogden that he met her at his waiting room "one minute too early", and she asked him to please not do so, otherwise she would not be able to know where she was (Ogden, 2024b, p. 288).

With time, the patient trusted the analyst enough to tell him that, for years, she had been sexually abused as a child by her uncle. These recollections are often perceived, by therapists, as 'memories', but Ogden offers a different perspective: to view them as *constructs within the present, mutually created by the analytic pair.* Of course, these 'constructs' are grounded in past events, but this should be of little interest to the analyst, claims Ogden: Whatever past events may have been, their relevance lies in the *here and now* of the analytic relationship and in the way they are co-constructed by the analytic pair. It takes time and effort, for both patient and analyst, to agree and be able *to live together these experiences,* and it takes time for the patient to be able to let go of this experience of *living together,* and to embark on the journey, by her- or himself. As much as the patient and the analyst may be *living an experience together,* eventually the patient can acknowledge and accept that the analyst *shares* and cares about her or his pain, but that is her or his pain. Nonetheless, the patient's ability to live an experience, together with the analyst, is vital for her or his ability to be on her or his own. It happens, perhaps, at such a moment that the analytic synchronic time is altered and becomes diachronic time, in which patient and analyst are two separate subjects.

In one of his most recent papers, "Inventing psychoanalysis with each patient", Ogden (2025, to be published) posits that *"for an analytic treatment to be alive and effective, the analyst must invent psychoanalysis with each patient" (p. 2, italics in original).* This requires that an analyst develops a personal "analytic style", grounded in each one's "freedom to create a form of psycho-analysis that will facilitate psychic change for each patient" (p. 2). Ogden then goes on to describe his own process of *becoming a psychoanalyst*, a process influenced by his long career of writing and teaching psychoanalysis:

> The three weekly seminars I conduct have each been going for more than 40 years. In these seminars, I sometimes speak as if I know what I am talking about, when in truth, I am talking about ideas and perspectives that are coming to me (through the work of the group) as I speak. The ideas I come to in these seminars form the basis of the analytic papers and books I write. In writing, too, I do not write what I think, I think what I write. For me, the process of writing is a critical part of becoming a psychoanalyst.
>
> (p. 5)

The process of *becoming* is a lifelong process, whether it is the process of *becoming a psychoanalyst, a teacher or a writer.* It is a process of *revelations* of one's thinking, based on one's *experiencing.* In this process, Ogden suggests, each analyst must carve out her or his own definition of what psychoanalytic thinking *is.* One of the concepts, fundamental to psychoanalytic thinking, that Ogden is concerned with is the concept of the 'unconscious'. The 'unconscious' is central to the thinking of most psychoanalytic theorists, beginning with Freud, Klein, and Fairbairn. Yet, this concept has undergone a profound change, following Winnicott's and Bion's thinking, leading to the ability to perceive the 'unconscious' more as an idea than as a 'fact'. This change is grounded in a significant change in psychoanalytic intervention, altering the discourse of contemporary psychoanalysis, from one based on the analyst's *interpretations* and the position of asserted *knowledge* to a discourse based on a joint *journey* of searching for personal meanings. In the latter, the analyst's position is not that of *knowing* and/or *understanding,* but more of a co-searcher, aiding the patient's process of *becoming who she or he really is:*

> Currently, I conceive of psychoanalysis as a discipline not only dealing with unconscious phenomena but also dealing with one's sense of what it is to be alive; one's sense of oneself as real; one's feeling of being an evolving person with a sense of self that feels continuous; one's experience of oneself as physically and imaginatively alive. The question of whether a particular state of mind is conscious, or unconscious seems to me not to be relevant to such states as feeling alive or feeling real or feeling present in one's own life. Aliveness is a feeling state, an emotional phenomenon; one feels it to one degree or another. It does not lend itself to being thought of as either possessing or not possessing conscious or unconscious qualities.
>
> (p. 7)

Perceiving psychoanalysis as, first and foremost, an *emotional endeavour,* is a reference to Winnicott's alteration of the human's development process as an *emotional process,* in which the baby's most vital achievement is that of *becoming a subject* (Winnicott 1958, 1965). This requires an early phase in which the mother lends the baby her own subjectivity as a means of ensuring the baby's state of *going-on-being,* a state in which the baby can be oblivious to any external phenomena, maintaining a serene psycho-mental state. Ogden posits that: "A good deal of psychic disturbance has its origins in circumstances in which the infant or child is unable to live his experience, which was too painful or disturbing or confusing when it occurred" (Ogden, 2025, p. 8).

Babies or young children may often be presented with circumstances that are beyond their psychic, emotional, or mental capacities, such as maternal depression, or the need to be apart from their mother (or father) too early. Such conditions may be a burden too heavy for the child, not allowing it *to experience* the situation emotionally. Ogden (2016c) refers to such circumstances or periods in the child's life as conditions that do not allow the child to *be alive*, or to experience them with *aliveness*, in a way that hinders the child's ability to *learn from that experience*:

> One is left with *a sense of internal emptiness, absence, and futility. Unlived life* is not an unconscious phenomenon, it is the atmosphere in which one lives, it *is a sense that one does not exist, a sense that one has no internal life, and hence no history and no future.*
>
> (p. 8, italics added)

Those *unlived experiences* become as-if 'holes' in one's psychic life, devoid of sense of *aliveness* and personal *meaning*. It is this idea that shapes Ogden's thinking of what contemporary psycho-analysis is about:

> It seems to me that at the core of every analysis is the ana-lyst's *evolving recognition* of who the patient is and who he or she is *becoming*. A good deal of the psychic change facilitated by analysis has its origins in communicating this recognition to the patient. Recognition derives from an unfolding under-standing of the patient, but *the analyst need not directly com-municate this understanding to the patient in words.* The analyst's understanding of the patient is experienced by the patient through many forms of verbal and nonverbal communication.
>
> (pp. 9–10, italics added)

In this paragraph, Ogden states some of his most important ideas on psychoanalysis and psychoanalytic treatment: (1) The main goal of psychoanalysis and psychoanalytic treatment is to facil-itate the *becoming of the patient*, meaning, helping the patient to *be who she or he really is;* (2) this is an evolving process; (3) although psychoanalysis and psychoanalytic treatment have to do with *understanding* what is happening; (4) this *understanding* should not be communicated in words; but rather (5) the analyst should facilitate the conditions in which the *patient can experience the analyst's understandings.*

Much of what goes on in the sessions and of what allows the psychic growth of the patient lies in the *experiences* and in the patient's and analyst's ability for *experiencing*. To this Ogden (1994) has referred to as the 'analytic third'; it is where the patient and analyst *live together an experience*, a space of *dreaming* and *playing*. Bion (1962b) has emphasised *dreaming,* while asleep *and* awake, as crucial to one's ability to do psychological work, and it is the patient's and analyst's ability of *dreaming together* that matters the most—it is their way of *living an experience together.* For Winnicott (1971a), psychoanalysis is about *playing* and psychoanalytic treatment is about the patient's and analyst's ability for *playing together:'*

> He [Winnicott] sees playing, like dreaming, as inherently psychotherapeutic so the analyst usually need not interpret in order to facilitate psychic growth, which Winnicott (1971c) describes as "a loosening of the knot and a forward movement in the developmental process" (p. 5).
>
> (Ogden, 1994, p. 10)

Ogden (2025) has made clear that ontological psychoanalysis does not exclude *understanding*. Nonetheless, "understanding must ride the wave of experience" (p. 11) and he emphasises the significance of the patient arriving at the understandings on her or his own. The analyst's role is to enable the experiences that can facilitate those understandings. Such experiences are extremely personal and different to each patient, and it requires the analyst to 'invent' psychoanalysis anew, for each patient. For this to be possible, says Ogden, each analyst must ask: "What does it mean to be a psychoanalyst?" or "What does it mean to practice psychoanalysis?"

Ogden's answer to these questions is that psychoanalysis is, first and foremost, a process in which a patient and an analyst *are living together experiences that the patient has not been able to fully live,* or that the patient has formerly been *living them alone.*

Psychoanalytic treatment is framed by the setting (the "analytic frame," Bleger, 1967), but Ogden admits to being open to some alterations in the framed setting, if these alterations can facilitate the patient's psychic growth. The analyst's 'presence', is different than the presence of a person who is not professionally or analytically trained, because it includes *knowledge* that others may not have.

Ogden (2025)gives an example of treating a rape survivor. Even in cases in which the analyst chooses to not interpret, her or his *way of being present* with this patient may include the analyst's familiarity with the work of: "Winnicott's concepts (1956) of disruption of 'going on being' (1949, p. 245) and fear of breakdown (1974), Shengold's concept of 'soul murder' (1989), Bion's account of 'psychic death' (1982), and myriads of other analytic concepts and clinical experiences" (Ogden, 2025, p. 480).

Each analyst may (and should) have certain rules that she or he follows, such as regarding physical touch (holding a patient's hand, for example). These rules serve as basic guidelines for our professional work and are based on our training and on our personal style. Yet, under some circumstances, some of these rules may be re-considered, which allows us to work differently with each of our patients. Under specific, perhaps unusual, circumstances, we may hold a patient's hand, give a patient a hug, meet a patient in her or his own house, see a patient over the weekend. Perhaps the best answer to the question "Is this good psychoanalytic practice?" is "It depends".

A simple solution for many psychoanalysts may be to always follow the rules and ethics we were taught. And indeed, most of these rules are grounded in good reasoning and have been set to protect patients from misconducts and analysts from being too confused. Ogden, in this paper, covers many of the conflicts that analysts experience in our daily practice of psychoanalysis. Yet, he proposes, bravely, to re-examine each rule, technique, or existing understanding and knowledge, with each of our patients:

> It is essential, if an analysis is to feel personal to the patient and to me, that the patient and I create a form of psychoanalysis unique to that patient. In the clinical illustrations I have presented, no other analyst would have conducted

himself precisely as I did. This is the way it should be and must be. That is part of what makes the analyst's inventing psychoanalysis with each patient a profound act of recognizing the patient for who he or she is.

(p. 25)

Epilogue
Beyond Understanding - The Revolution in Psychoanalytic Experience

In the spring of 2025, as I put the finishing touches on this exploration of Thomas Ogden's ontological psychoanalysis, I found myself returning to a question that has haunted me throughout this writing: What does it mean to truly *be* with another person in their suffering and transformation? This question, which sits at the heart of Ogden's revolutionary contribution to psychoanalytic thought, feels both ancient and urgently contemporary.

Writing this book has been, in many ways, an exercise in ontological psychoanalysis itself. Like the analytic process Ogden describes the act of engaging with his work has required me to move beyond the comfortable realm of understanding into the more uncertain territory of experiencing. I have found myself changed not merely by what I have learned about Ogden's ideas, but by the process of allowing those ideas to work on me, to reshape my own way of being present with patients, students, and the written word itself.

The journey through Ogden's thinking—from his early reconceptualization of projective identification and the analytic third, through his profound readings of psychoanalytic ancestors, to his mature articulation of ontological psychoanalysis—reveals a consistent thread: the primacy of lived experience over theoretical understanding. This is not an anti-intellectual stance, but rather a recognition that *genuine transformation occurs in the realm of being*, not merely knowing.

DOI: 10.4324/9781003388708-6

The Courage to Not Know

What strikes me most profoundly about Ogden's work is the courage it requires—not the courage to know, but *the courage to not know*. In a professional field that has often prided itself on expertise, interpretation, and the analyst's ability to unlock unconscious meanings, Ogden invites us into a fundamentally different relationship with knowledge itself. This shift demands what he calls 'self-renunciation', a willingness to abandon the security of professional identity in favour of authentic encounter.

I think of the analyst who said "I love you" to Ms. C when love was what the moment demanded, or the simple response "Of course you are" to a terrified patient's acknowledgment of her fear. These are not interventions born of theoretical sophistication, but of a deeper wisdom—the wisdom of presence that trusts the transformative power of genuine human contact. Such moments reveal psychoanalysis not as a technique for understanding pathology, but as an art form dedicated to facilitating authentic being.

This courage to inhabit uncertainty extends to Ogden's relationship with psychoanalytic tradition itself. Rather than dismissing the contributions of Freud, Klein, Winnicott, and Bion, he demonstrates how each generation must "kill" its ancestors in order to give birth to something genuinely new. This is not the murderous destruction that eliminates the past, but the creative destruction that honours tradition while transcending it. In his hands, Winnicott's concept of "going-on-being" converses with Bion's theory of thinking; Klein's understanding of projective identification finds new life in the context of intersubjective experience.

The Poetry of Psychoanalytic Encounter

Perhaps nowhere is Ogden's genius more evident than in his integration of literary sensibility with clinical wisdom. His discussions of Frost's poetry, his exploration of Borges' (1941–2) labyrinthine narratives, his attention to the music of language itself—all reveal a practitioner who understands that psychoanalysis, at its deepest level, is a poetic endeavour. The analyst's task is not merely to decode symptoms or interpret transferences, but to participate in the creation of a living text, whose meaning emerges through the very act of being written together.

This poetic dimension of Ogden's work challenges the increasing medicalization of psychotherapy. While evidence-based practices focus on measurable outcomes and standardized interventions, Ogden reminds us that the most profound changes in human life occur in dimensions that resist quantification. How do we measure the moment when a patient first feels real to her or himself? How do we standardize the process by which someone moves from existing to truly living?

The concept of 'unlived life', which threads through Ogden's later work, offers a particularly poignant example of this poetic understanding. The idea that we carry within ourselves experiences too overwhelming to be fully lived when they occurred speaks to something fundamental about human temporality and the possibility of psychological redemption. Analysis becomes a space where the past can be experienced for the first time, where what was unthinkable can finally be thought, where the unlived can be brought into being.

This is psychoanalysis as archaeology of the soul—not simply uncovering what was buried, but *creating conditions where what was too disturbing to be experienced can finally be lived*. The analyst serves not as an expert interpreter of hidden meanings, but as a companion willing to enter the darkness of trauma and neglect, trusting that her or his presence can help create space for new possibilities.

The Dialectic of Solitude and Togetherness

One of the most sophisticated aspects of Ogden's thinking lies in his understanding of the dialectical nature of human experience. The concept of the 'analytic third' exemplifies this beautifully—a space that belongs to neither analyst nor patient, yet emerges from their unconscious collaboration. This paradoxical space, where two people can be simultaneously separate and joined, individual and merged, captures something essential about the human condition itself.

We are beings who require both solitude and connection, who need to be seen and recognized while maintaining what Winnicott called the 'incommunicado self'. Ogden's work navigates this paradox with remarkable sensitivity, showing how genuine intimacy depends upon the preservation of separateness, how authentic meeting requires the capacity to be alone in the presence of another.

This *dialectical understanding* extends to the relationship between understanding and experience, which permeates all of Ogden's work. He does not dismiss the importance of insight or interpretation but rather insists that understanding must 'ride the wave of experience'. Knowledge that emerges from lived encounter has a quality entirely different from knowledge imposed by theoretical frameworks. It is knowledge that transforms the knower in the very process of being known.

The Revolutionary Implications

The revolution that Ogden represents is, in many ways, a quiet one. It does not announce itself with grand manifestos or dramatic technical innovations. Instead, it manifests in subtle shifts of emphasis: from interpretation to presence, from understanding to experiencing, from knowing to being. Yet these seemingly modest changes have profound implications for how we conceive of psychoanalytic work and human transformation more generally.

Consider the implications for training and supervision. Ogden's approach suggests that the most important capacities—the ability to reverie, to tolerate uncertainty, to remain present in the face of disturbing material—cannot be taught in any conventional sense. But how do we teach someone to practice ontological psychoanalysis? The implications extend beyond training to the very identity of psychoanalysis as a discipline. In an era of increasing specialization and professionalization, Ogden's work reminds us that psychoanalysis, at its core, is not a medical treatment, but a form of human encounter that has the potential to transform both participants. This understanding challenges the medicalization of psychological suffering while offering a vision of healing that goes far beyond symptom reduction to touch something essential about what it means to be fully human.

The Challenge of Authenticity

Running through all of Ogden's work is a concern with *authenticity*—the question of *what it means to be real, to feel alive, to inhabit one's own existence with genuine presence*. This concern feels particularly urgent in our current cultural moment, where social media and digital connectivity often substitute virtual interaction for genuine encounter, where the pace of modern life leaves little space for the kind of deep reflection and emotional processing that Ogden's work requires.

The patients who populate Ogden's clinical vignettes often struggle with a profound sense of unreality, a feeling of being visitors in their own lives. Ms. C, who experienced herself as "in the wrong place" when she came to analysis, or Mr. V, who couldn't feel that his house was his house or that his family were truly his family—these individuals embody a form of existential suffering that cannot be addressed through symptom-focused interventions alone.

What they need, Ogden suggests, is not explanation or interpretation, but recognition—the experience of being truly seen and met by another human being. This recognition cannot be manufactured or applied as a technique; it emerges from the analyst's willingness to be authentically present, to risk a genuine encounter, to abandon the safety of professional distance in favour of human contact.

The Future of Psychoanalytic Experience

As I reflect on the clinical vignettes scattered throughout Ogden's work, I am struck by their luminous quality—the way they capture moments of authentic human contact that feel both extraordinary and utterly ordinary. These are not case studies designed to illustrate theoretical points, but rather invitations into the sacred space where two people encounter each other's fundamental humanity. In Ms. L's terror at beginning analysis, in Mr. C's dream of washing his car with cerebral palsy, in the analyst's willingness to say "I love you" when love is what the moment calls for—we witness psychoanalysis stripped of its professional pretensions and revealed as something far more precious: the art of being genuinely present with another's truth.

What emerges from this survey of Ogden's work is not a new technique or therapeutic approach in any conventional sense, but rather an invitation to a different way of being an analyst—and perhaps, a different way of being human. The analyst who practices ontological psychoanalysis must be willing to abandon the safety of professional expertise in favour of a more vulnerable encounter with the unknown. This requires what Ogden calls 'self-renunciation'—not a self-destructive giving up of oneself, but a creative willingness to become "less definitively oneself" in service of something larger.

The concept of the analytic third, which runs like a golden thread through all of Ogden's work, represents perhaps his most significant contribution to psychoanalytic theory. By recognizing that genuine analytic work occurs in a space that belongs fully to neither analyst nor patient but emerges from their unconscious collaboration, Ogden has provided a theoretical framework for understanding how transformation actually occurs. *The analytic third* is not a technique to be applied but *a state of being* to be cultivated—a willingness to participate in the creation of something genuinely new.

Looking toward the future, Ogden's work offers both hope and challenge for psychoanalysis as a discipline. The hope lies in his demonstration that psychoanalytic thinking can remain alive and creative, that each generation can discover something genuinely new while honouring what came before. His willingness to "invent psychoanalysis with each patient," to read familiar texts as if encountering them for the first time, to allow understanding to emerge from experience rather than imposing predetermined frameworks—all of this models a way of practicing and thinking about psychoanalysis that keeps it vital and relevant.

The challenge lies in the demands this approach makes on practitioners. *Ontological psychoanalysis cannot be reduced to techniques or protocols.* It requires a fundamental orientation toward being that must be cultivated over time through personal analysis, clinical experience, and ongoing self-reflection. It asks analysts to remain vulnerable to surprise, to tolerate the anxiety of not knowing, to trust in the transformative power of authentic encounter even when external pressures push toward more measurable and standardized approaches.

Implications Beyond the Consulting Room

The implications of Ogden's ontological turn extend far beyond the consulting room into broader questions about human development, education, and the possibility of authentic relationships in contemporary culture. His insights about the importance of being seen and recognized, about the need for spaces where genuine playing and dreaming can occur, about the transformative power of presence over interpretation—all of these have relevance for how we think about parenting, teaching, friendship, and love.

In our increasingly achievement-oriented culture, where children are often pushed toward external accomplishments rather than authentic self-discovery, Ogden's emphasis on 'going-on-being' offers a necessary corrective. The question "What do you want to be when you grow up?" which provides the subtitle for his seminal paper on ontological psychoanalysis, points toward something more fundamental than career choices or life goals. It asks about the quality of being itself, about what it means to inhabit one's own existence with authenticity and aliveness.

This has profound implications for how we understand mental health and psychological well-being. Rather than focusing primarily on symptom reduction or behavioural change, an ontological approach asks whether someone feels real to themselves, whether they experience their life as genuinely their own, whether they have access to their own creativity and capacity for growth. These may seem like luxuries in a world focused on basic functioning and survival, but Ogden's work suggests they are necessities—that without a sense of authentic being, even apparent health becomes a form of sophisticated false self-organization.

The concept of 'unlived life' speaks to a form of psychological suffering that is rarely addressed in conventional therapeutic approaches. How many people carry within themselves dreams that were never allowed to unfold, aspects of personality that were suppressed in service of adaptation, capacities for joy and creativity that were sacrificed to the demands of survival? Ontological psychoanalysis offers the possibility that these buried potentials can be recovered and brought to life, even decades after they were first sacrificed.

The Question of Training and Education

If we take Ogden's insights seriously, they raise fundamental questions about how psychoanalysts are trained and how psychoanalytic knowledge is transmitted. Traditional analytic education has focused heavily on theory acquisition, case presentation, and the development of interpretive skills. But how do we teach someone to tolerate uncertainty, to trust their reveries, to remain present in the face of disturbing material? These qualities must be cultivated through experience, modelled through relationships, discovered through one's own analysis and clinical work.

Ogden's approach suggests that the most important learning in psychoanalytic training happens not in the classroom but in the consulting room, not through theoretical study but through lived experience. This points toward a more apprenticeship-based model of psychoanalytic education, one that emphasizes the development of being over the acquisition of knowledge. It suggests that the most important question for candidates is not "What do you understand about psychoanalysis?" but rather "Who are you becoming through your engagement with this work?"

Yet this creates its own challenges. How do we ensure quality and consistency in training if so much depends on ineffable qualities like presence and authenticity? How do we maintain standards while honouring the deeply personal nature of analytic development? These are questions that the psychoanalytic community will need to grapple with as it integrates the insights of ontological psychoanalysis into its educational practices.

The role of personal analysis in training becomes even more central from this perspective. If the analysts' primary tool is their own being—their capacity for reverie, their ability to tolerate uncertainty, their willingness to be affected by their patients—then the depth and quality of their own analytic experience becomes paramount. This is not simply about resolving personal conflicts or understanding one's own dynamics, but about developing the capacity for authentic presence that Ogden's work describes.

The Challenge of Evidence and Efficacy

Ogden's ontological approach also poses significant challenges for a field increasingly concerned with evidence-based practice and measurable outcomes. How do we study or evaluate the effectiveness of an approach that resists standardization? How do we measure aliveness, authenticity, or the capacity to feel real? These are not trivial questions in an era where healthcare systems demand proof of efficacy and cost-effectiveness.

Yet Ogden's work suggests that some of the most important aspects of human transformation may be precisely those that resist measurement. The moment when a patient first feels genuinely seen, the gradual development of the capacity to play, the slow emergence of authentic voice—these changes may be profoundly life-altering while remaining largely invisible to conventional outcome measures.

This creates a tension that the psychoanalytic community must navigate carefully. On one hand, there is value in demonstrating that psychoanalytic treatment can produce meaningful change and justify the investment of time and resources it requires. On the other hand, reducing psychoanalysis to measurable outcomes may fundamentally alter its nature, transforming an art form dedicated to facilitating authentic being into a technology for producing predetermined results.

As I bring this exploration to a close, I am aware that I have not 'explained' Thomas Ogden in any definitive sense. Like the dreams and reveries he writes about so eloquently, his work resists final interpretation. Instead, I hope I have created something more valuable: an invitation for readers to encounter Ogden's thinking in their own way, to allow it to work on them as it has worked on me, to discover for themselves what it might mean to practice an ontological psychoanalysis.

In our increasingly disconnected world, where genuine human encounter becomes ever rarer and more precious, the vision of psychoanalysis that emerges from Ogden's work feels both necessary and hopeful. It suggests that transformation remains possible, that the capacity for authentic being can be recovered and cultivated, and that the simple act of two people meeting each other with honesty and courage retains its power to heal and transform.

The final word, perhaps, should go to Ogden himself, whose understanding of psychoanalysis as a fundamentally creative endeavour points toward something essential about human nature:

"The analyst must learn anew how to be an analyst with each patient in each session" (Ogden, 2004b, p. 862).

Psychoanalysis is a profoundly personal journey of both patient and analyst, a unique *creation* of both. We are not merely the products of our past experiences, not simply the bearers of symptoms to be treated or problems to be solved. We are beings capable of *continuous becoming*, of *dreaming ourselves into fuller existence*, of *creating meaning* through the very act of living. Psychoanalysis, as Ogden practices and envisions it, is a (transitional) space where this fundamental creativity can be honoured, protected, and set free.

In the end, this is what I take from my engagement with Thomas Ogden's revolutionary vision: an invitation to approach each encounter—whether with a patient, a text, or life itself—with the kind of presence that makes transformation possible. It is an invitation to move beyond the safety of understanding into the more dangerous and fertile territory of genuine experience. It is, ultimately, an invitation to become more fully human.

Ofrit Shapira-Berman
May 2025

References

Bick, E. (1968). The experience of the skin in early object relations. *The International Journal of Psychoanalysis*, 49: pp. 484–486.

Bion, W. R. (1959). Attacks on linking. *The International Journal of Psychoanalysis*, 40: pp. 308–315.

Bion, W. R. (1962a). *Learning from experience*. New York: Basic Books.

Bion, W. R. (1962b). 'A theory of thinking'. In: Aronson, J. (1967). *Second Thoughts*. New York: Inc., pp. 110–119.

Bion, W. R. (1962c). The psychoanalytic study of thinking. *The International Journal of Psychoanalysis*, 53: pp. 306–310.

Bion, W. R. (1967). Notes on memory and desire. In: Bion, W. (2013). *Los Angeles Seminars and Supervision*, ed. J. Aguayo & B. Malin. London: Karnac, pp. 136–138.

Bion, W. R. (1970). *Attention and interpretation*. New York: Aronson.

Bion, W. R. (1982). *The Long Weekend: 1897–1919 (Part of a Life)*, ed. F. Bion, Abingdon: The Fleetwood Press.

Bleger, J. (1967). 'Psychoanalysis of the psychoanalytic setting'. Chapter 6 in Churcher J. & L. Bleger, eds. (2013). *Symbiosis and Ambiguity*. London: Routledge.

Borges, J. L. (1941–1942). Ficciones. Buenos Aires: Editorial Sur. English Translation: *Fictions* (1962). New York: Grove Press.

Chomsky, N. (1957). *Syntactic Structures*. The Hague: Mouton.

Chomsky, N. (1968). Linguistic contributions to the study of mind: Future. *Language and thinking*, pp. 323–364.

Freud, A. (1936). *The ego and the mechanisms of defence*. New York: International Universities Press.

Freud, S. (1915). *Instincts and their vicissitudes*. Standard Edition, 14: pp. 117–140.

Freud, S. (1920). *Beyond the pleasure principle*. Standard Edition, 18: pp. 7–66.

Frost, R. (1917). Letter to Louis Untermeyer, 1 Jan. 1917. In: Pritchard, W. (1984). *Frost: A Literary Life Reconsidered*. Amherst: University of Massachusetts Press.

Frost, R. (1930). Education by poetry. In: Porirer, R., Richardson, M., eds. (1995). *Robert Frost: Collected poems, prose and plays*. New York: Library of America, pp. 717–728.

Frost, R. (1995). *Collected Poems, Prose and Plays*. New York: Library of America.

Grotstein, J. S. (1980a). The significance of Kleinian contributions to psychoanalysis I. Kleinian instinct theory. *Int. J. Psychoanal. Psychother.*, 8: pp. 375–392.

Grotstein, J. S. (1980b). The significance of Kleinian contributions to psychoanalysis II. Freudian and Kleinian conceptions of early mental development. *Int. J. Psychoanal. Psychother.*, 8: pp. 393–428.

Grotstein, J. S. (1981). *Do I Dare Disturb the Universe?* New York: Routledge.

Grotstein, J. S. (1984). A proposed revision of the psychoanalytic concept of primitive mental states, Part II. *Contemporary Psychoanalysis*, 20 (2): pp. 266–343.

Isaacs, S. (1952). The nature and function of phantasy. In: Klein. M. *et al.* (eds.) *Developments in Psycho-Analysis*. London: Hogarth Press, pp. 67–121.

Klein, M. (1952a). Some theoretical conclusions regarding the emotional life of the infant. In: (1946–1963). *Envy and Gratitude and Other Works*. New York: Delacorte Press, pp. 61–93.

Loewald, H. W. (1979). The waning of the Oedipus complex. *Journal of the American Psychoanalytic Association*, 27 (4): pp. 751–775.

Meltzer, D. (1975). *Explorations in Autism*. Perthshire: Clunie Press.

Ogden, T. H. (1979a). On projective identification. *The International Journal of Psychoanalysis*, 60 (3): pp. 357–373.

Ogden, T. H. (1979b). Reverie and interpretation. *The Psychoanalytic Quarterly*, 66 (4): pp. 567–595.

Ogden, T. H. (1984). Instinct, phantasy, and psychological deep structure: A reinterpretation of aspects of the work of Melanie Klein. *Contemporary Psychoanalysis*, 20 (4): pp. 500–525.

Ogden, T. H. (1985). On potential space. *The International Journal of Psychoanalysis*, 66: pp. 129–141.

Ogden, T. H. (1994). The Analytic Third—Working with Intersubjective Clinical Facts. *The International Journal of Psychoanalysis*, 75: pp. 3–19.

Ogden, T. H. (1996). The perverse subject of analysis. *Journal of the American Psychoanalytic Association*, 44 (4): pp. 1121–1146.

Ogden, T. H. (1997a). Some thoughts on the use of language in psycho-analysis. *Psychoanalytic Dialogues*, 7 (1): pp. 1–21.

Ogden, T. H. (1997b). Listening three Frost poems. *Psychoanalytic Dialogues*, 7 (5): pp. 619–639.

Ogden, T. H. (1997c). Reverie and interpretation. *The Psychoanalytic Quarterly*, 66 (4): pp. 567–595.

Ogden, T. H. (1998). A question of voice in poetry and psychoanalysis. *The Psychoanalytic Quarterly*, 67 (3): pp. 426–448.

Ogden, T. H. (2001). Reading Winnicott. *The Psychoanalytic Quarterly*, 70 (2): pp. 299–323.

Ogden, T. H. (2003). On not being able to dream. *The International Journal of Psychoanalysis*, 84 (1): pp. 17–30.

Ogden, T. H. (2004a). An introduction to the reading of Bion. *The International Journal of Psychoanalysis*, 85 (2): pp. 285–300.

Ogden, T. H. (2004b). This art of psychoanalysis: Dreaming undreamt dreams and interrupted cries. *The International Journal of Psycho-analysis*, 85: pp. 857–877.

Ogden, T. H. (2004c). The analytic third: Implications for psychoanalytic theory and technique. *The Psychoanalytic Quarterly*, 73 (1): pp. 167–195.

Ogden, T. H. (2004d). On holding and containing, being and dreaming. *The International Journal of Psychoanalysis*, 85 (6): pp. 1349–1364.

Ogden, T. H. (2006). Reading Loewald: Oedipus reconceived. *The International Journal of Psychoanalysis*, 87 (3): pp. 651–666.

Ogden, T. H. (2007). Reading Harold Searles. *The International Journal of Psychoanalysis*, 88 (2): pp. 353–369.

Ogden, T. H. (2009). Rediscovering psychoanalysis. *Psychoanalytic Perspectives*, 6 (1): pp. 22–31.

Ogden, T. H. (2010). Why read Fairbairn? *The International Journal of Psychoanalysis*, 91 (1): pp. 101–118.

Ogden, T. H. (2011). Reading Susan Isaacs: Towards a radically revised theory of thinking. *The Psychoanalytic Quarterly*, 80: pp. 925–947.

Ogden, T. H. (2014). Fear of breakdown and the unlived life. *The International Journal of Psychoanalysis*, 95 (2): pp. 205–223.

Ogden, T. H. (2015). Intuiting the truth of what's happening: On Bion's "Notes on memory and desire". *The Psychoanalytic Quarterly*, 84 (2): pp. 285–306.

Ogden, T. H. (2016a). Destruction reconceived: On Winnicott's 'The use of an object and relating through identifications'. *The International Journal of Psychoanalysis*, 97 (5): pp. 1243–1262.

Ogden, T. H. (2016b). Some thoughts on practicing psychoanalysis. *Fort Da*, 22 (1): pp. 21–36.

Ogden, T. H. (2016c). *Reclaiming Unlived Life: Experiences in Psychoanalysis* (New Library of Psychoanalysis). London: Routledge.

Ogden, T. H. (2018a). 'The analytic third: Working with intersubjective clinical facts'. In: *The Analytic Field*. London: Routledge, pp. 159–188.

Ogden, T. H. (2018b). 'The music of what happens in poetry and psychoanalysis'. In: *Key Papers in Literature and Psychoanalysis*. London: Routledge, pp. 49–76.

Ogden, T. H. (2018c). How I talk with my patients. *The Psychoanalytic Quarterly*, 87 (3): pp. 399–413.

Ogden, T. H. (2019). Ontological psychoanalysis or 'What do you want to be when you grow up?'. *The Psychoanalytic Quarterly*, 88 (4): pp. 661–684.

Ogden, T. H. (2024a). Ontological psychoanalysis in clinical practice. *The Psychoanalytic Quarterly*, 93 (1): pp. 13–31.

Ogden, T. H. (2024b). Rethinking the concepts of the unconscious and analytic time. *The International Journal of Psychoanalysis*, 105 (3): pp. 279–291.

Ogden, T. H. (2025). Inventing psychoanalysis with each patient. *The International Journal of Psychoanalysis* (to be published).

Segal, H. (1957). Notes on symbol formation. *The International Journal of Psychoanalysis*, 38: pp. 391–397.

Shengold, L. (1989). *Soul Murder: The Effects of Childhood Abuse and Deprivation*. New York, NY: Random House.

Symington, N. (1983). The analyst's freedom to think as agent of therapeutic change. *International Review of Psychoanalysis*, 10: pp. 283–291.

Tustin, F. (1972). *Autism and Childhood Psychosis*. London: Hogarth Press.

Winnicott, D. W. (1945). Primitive emotional development. *The International Journal of Psychoanalysis*, 26: p. 137.

Winnicott, D. W. (1949). 'Mind and its relation to the psyche-soma'. In: (1958). *Through Paediatrics to Psychoanalysis*. New York, NY: Basic Books, pp. 243–254.

Winnicott, D. W. (1956). 'Primary maternal preoccupation'. In: (1958). *Through Paediatrics to Psychoanalysis*. New York, NY: Basic Books, pp. 300–305.

Winnicott, D. W. (1958). *Through Paediatrics to Psychoanalysis*. New York, NY: Basic Books.

Winnicott, D. W. (1960). 'The theory of the parent-infant relationship'. In: *The Maturational Processes and the Facilitating Environment*. New York: International Universities Press, pp. 37–55.

Winnicott, D. W. (1962). The theory of the parent-infant relationship: further remarks. *The International Journal of Psychoanalysis*, 43: p. 238.

Winnicott, D. W. (1963). 'Communicating and not communicating leading to a study of certain opposites'. In: (1965). *The Maturational Processes and the Facilitating Environment*. New York: International Universities Press, pp. 179–192.

Winnicott, D. W. (1965). *The Maturational Forces and the Facilitating Environment*. New York, NY: International Universities Press.

Winnicott, D. W. (1971a) 'Playing: A theoretical statement'. In: *Playing and Reality*. New York: Basic Books, pp. 38–52.

Winnicott, D. W. (1971b). 'Transitional objects and transitional phenomena'. In: *Playing and Reality*. New York: Basic Books, pp. 1–25.

Winnicott, D. W. (1971c). *Therapeutic Consultations in Child Psychiatry*. New York, NY: Basic Books.

Winnicott, D. W. (1974). Fear of breakdown. *Int Rev. Psychoanal.*, 1: pp. 103–107.

Winnicott D. W. (2007). 'The use of an object and relating through identifications'. In: *Playing and reality*. New York, NY: Basic Books, pp. 86–94.

Index

A

Aliveness/Being alive
as central to psychoanalysis, 7,
39, 62–64, 77–79, 90–91
vs. deadness, 63
dreaming and, 39–42
language and, 62–64
ontological emphasis on, 1,
76–82
reverie and, 8
true self and, 37, 63

Alpha-function (Bion)
definition and role, 39–40
dreaming and, 40–41, 81–82
mother's provision of, 81–82
transformation of beta-elements,
39–40

Analytic frame/setting
alterations in, 93
analyst's hatred expressed
through, 36–37
basic guidelines, 93

Analytic style
personal creation of, 71, 89, 93–94
uniqueness with each patient,
70–72, 89, 93–94

Analytic third
clinical illustrations, 12–14
co-creation by analyst and
patient, 3, 7–8, 14–15

definition and characteristics,
7–8, 14–15
dialectical nature, 7–8
intersubjective space, xii, 3, 14,
56
paradoxical nature, 8, 12
projective identification and,
6, 14
reverie and, 12–14, 56
shared psychological realm, 56,
64, 92

Analytic time
diachronic vs. synchronic, 86–89
dream time, 86–87
past as alive in present, 87–88

Analyst's role
being with vs. talking to patient,
35, 37
co-creation with patient, 91–94
containing function, 42–47
facilitating conditions for
growth, 1, 77–78, 91–92
holding function, 42–44
invention of psychoanalysis with
each patient, 89, 93–94
recognition of patient, 85–86, 91
self-renunciation, 55–56, 96, 100

Authenticity
challenge of, 99
voice and, 62–64
vs. true/false self, 63

For Product Safety Concerns and Information please contact our EU
representative GPSR@taylorandfrancis.com
Taylor & Francis Verlag GmbH, Kaufingerstraße 24, 80331 München, Germany

www.ingramcontent.com/pod-product-compliance
Lightning Source LLC
Chambersburg PA
CBHW071748270326
41928CB00013B/2839